True Stories of an Aging Do-Gooder

How cohousing can bridge cultural divides

By Alan O'Hashi

Boulder Community

Media (BCM)

Boulder Community Media (BCM)

BCM

**Creating the New
Creative Economy**

www.bouldercomedia.com

This book is a memoir. It reflects the author's present recollections of experiences over time. Some names and characteristics have been changed, some events have been compressed, and some dialogue has been recreated.

Boulder Community Media (BCM), Publisher
1650 Yellow Pine Avenue
Boulder, CO 80304

Second Printing – March 2024

Copyright © 2020

ISBN 979-8571039482

Dedication

While not a novel, I completed this memoir in November 2020, National Novel Writing Month, aka NaNoWriMo.

I excerpted part of the book for two *Communities Magazine* articles. The manuscript was written during the COVID-19 pandemic, and I updated the story.

If there was any benefit from being holed up in front of my computer screen during the pandemic, it was meeting writers from around the world in Zoom and Google Meetup rooms.

I learned that COVID or no COVID, I don't get out much.

Thanks to my writing friends and colleagues who convene daily to write down their thoughts and ideas on paper.

We are all accountable to each other.

Table of Contents

Forward: Stream of Consciousness

I've lived a life of divergent experiences that converged when I joined the Silver Sage Village (SSV) senior cohousing community in Boulder, Colorado.

SSV is one of 170 or so existing cohousing communities in the United States.

My story is a somewhat organized stream of consciousness about how to play well with others, particularly around collaboration methods among traditionally disenfranchised people and members of the dominant culture who are the typical residents of a cohousing community.

Rental and owner-occupied cohousing is one nexus of lower-priced housing and social change.

Intentional community members can share resources like time and money, whether owners or renters. They spread financial risks around while the community is operated and maintained collaboratively.

I'll offer a paradigm shift about how cohousing can bridge socio-economic divides.

In case you've just returned after several years in outer space, the COVID-19 pandemic that began in 2019 circled the globe and ended around 2022. The disease continues to infect people, but the frenzy has subsided.

At the height of the pandemic, everyone was obliged to stay inside to decrease the spread of the infection. Like everyone else, I had quite a bit of extra time on my hands.

I had no idea how my day was occupied before self-isolating in front of my computer, and still don't.

If you're a Baby Boomer or older, it's not the first pandemic we've experienced since the 1950s.

In the past, I helped stop polio and the swine flu by taking the vaccines. Stopping COVID-19 was no different. I dutifully and routinely have been jabbed by the updated medicine.

COVID-19 brought to light glaring cultural inequities. The pandemic closed down the economy, forcing employers to reduce their labor force.

That exposed the lack of lower-priced housing options when people lost their homes, particularly rental homes.

There was a domino effect that continued after the pandemic. At least in Colorado, COVID-19 evictions were prohibited, which was good for renters but not good for landlords.

The dominos started to fall even though the economy began to pick up. When rent relief funding ended, evictions rose and continue to be problematic in 2024.

A landlord may evict tenants, but the number of replacement renters is small since the same people are looking for less expensive housing.

For apartment and home owners who default on their loans, how will lenders at the top of the financial mountain that conglomerate mortgages as security pay their investors?

Remember the No Income No Jobs (NINJA) loans that caused the 2008 housing crisis? Home and car buyers with risky financial histories could qualify for loans if they had a credit score.

My partner, Diana, and I had a variable rate mortgage and refinanced with a NINJA loan. We filled out a form and soon had a lower interest rate when our loan was bought by a mortgage company that turned out to be one of the subprime mortgage bad players.

The COVID-19 housing crisis was the reverse of what happened in 2008. Working people with solid financial histories lost their jobs, too.

Related to housing, racial justice issues quickly floated to the top of the social change pond.

African American and Latine people were at a higher risk of contracting COVID-19, being hospitalized, and death than the general population. They were on the front lines, stocking grocery store shelves and providing support services in the healthcare industry.

The book is part "self-help" memoir and part "how-to" manual about my experiences that seemed unrelated at the time but added to my life gestalt, which eventually led me to believe cohousing can make social change happen by bridging cultural divides.

The story is written from my viewpoint as a cohousing community member, as opposed to that of a cohousing professional or a cohousing professional who lives in a community.

I offer methods about ways your community can use cultural competency techniques that encourage members to understand one another better, ways to deal with xenophobia toward traditionally marginalized racial and ethnic groups, and those based on gender self-identification.

Suppose you're looking for "hands-on" information about designing a Common House, how to lay out the garden, or pick a community governance method.

In that case, my book can help you create your community in a more inclusive manner.

The stories are about relations between and among individuals and the personal changes necessary to find commonality with people with different experiences and lifestyles.

Forming a cohousing community reminds me of a movie called *Lifeboat* (1944), based on a story by John Steinbeck directed by Alfred Hitchcock and stars Tallulah Bankhead and William Bendix.

A cruise ship and a German U-boat are sunk in a battle. A group of survivors ends up in the same lifeboat.

The movie explores the interpersonal relationships that develop in a confined space.

Conflicts arise between wealthy and poor members about essential items that should remain in the boat and who should be in charge.

The most significant decision is about what to do with the German sailor who is among the survivors.

They navigate their craft to the West Indies, and along the way, some die, but all reveal their true self-interested natures.

During the COVID-19 pandemic, I had extra time to sort through boxes and purge junk I hadn't handled for years.

I make movies and hauled a box of obsolete cameras, cables, and assorted production equipment to the only second-hand store in Boulder that accepted electronics. That was a big relief and a positive pandemic outcome for me.

Besides sorting my physical stuff, I decided to categorize blog posts, PowerPoint presentations from workshops, and talks I've presented over the past 40 years.

After getting up off my Silver Sage Village couch, all my sorted content turned into this book, *True Stories of an Aging Do-Gooder ... How cohousing bridges cultural divides* about the circumstances that transformed me into a cohousing disciple and how cohousing can be more accessible to all.

"That's a really great housing model. How come I haven't heard about it?" is a typical response I hear after striking up conversations with the curious.

Good question.

If cohousing is such a tremendous and earth-shattering idea, why aren't thousands of communities popping up in all corners of the country?

Another good question.

The book provides some insights.

I estimate that 30,000 people reside in an existing cohousing community, one in the community formation phase, or are just interested individuals.

Cohousing residents have high levels of resiliency because of the collaborative nature of each community.

Cohousers confronted COVID-19 head-on. What if they refocused that energy, became organized, and decided to collectively undertake a mission to save the world?

True Stories explores why I believe cohousing growth has been slowly steady and unprolific and offers some ideas about how cohousing can evolve from a "social movement" into being a "social norm."

The only person I have any control over is myself. Personal change happens when the length of time between the past and present is as short as possible.

Although I get wound up in day-to-day routines, writing this book spurred me to rewind the socialization tapes playing in my head, reflect on the past, and figure out how to shed my deeply ingrained behaviors.

That's a never-ending task since I wake up a different person every morning based on the previous day's events and interactions.

My experiences aren't that remarkable, but the intent is to encourage you to remember what happened in your personal history as you figure out the opportunities and challenges you'll face when choosing to care and share in a cohousing community.

Alan O'Hashi
Boulder, Colorado

Disclaimer

I also happen to be a member of the Cohousing Association of the U.S. (CohoUS) board of directors and Past President.

The opinions and ideas expressed in this story are mine and do not reflect the views of CohoUS or other organizations and individuals. No animals were harmed during the writing and publication of this book.

The large type size and extra white space are to accommodate Baby Boomer eyes.

Prologue: Get Up Off the Couch!

"Get Up Off the Couch" is a call to action.

The idea is to build a grassroots network of cohousing communities and their members, along with local, national, and global organizations and individuals.

Socio-economic divides widened during the COVID-19 pandemic. Cohousing is one solution that has the potential to narrow that gap.

What if cohousers get up off the couch and create cost-efficient housing options inclusive of marginalized and diverse people?

It's going to take more than self-expression, like ranting, chanting, raving, and waving signs at a rally to raise awareness.

Once the photo-ops have passed, and column inches on a blog post are forgotten by the next news cycle, not much social change has happened.

What if we all got off the couch and took the time to SHARE with others?

- Socialize – Get out there
- Help Out – Lend a hand up
- Accept – All have value as themselves
- Reach Out – Meet and greet with respect
- Engage – Do good, do no harm, be nice

Why is SHARE a good fit for cohousing and other intentional communities?

Remember the old 1950s TV show, *The Adventures of Superman*?

The narrator told my friends and me to model Superman's can-do behavior because "he fights a never-ending battle for truth, justice, and the American Way."

Superman's American Way is based on rugged individualism, cultural divides narrowed by assimilation, and quests for power and control.

By definition, cohousing communities and their members do their best to collaborate and put individual "self-interests" aside in favor of the good of the whole.

Theoretically, cohousers are inclusive and meet people where they are, and in many cases, share a common "higher purpose."

There isn't anything inherently wrong with Superman's "American Way," I think it needs to evolve along with society, and one way that can happen is through a collaborative approach.

Lincoln's Emancipation Proclamation happened in 1863 but wasn't enforced until 1865. A century later, President Lyndon Johnson signed the Civil Rights Act of 1964, followed by the Voting Rights Act in 1965.

Jim Crow law residue is still evident, and to this day, Congressional and state legislative districts are gerrymandered to disenfranchise Black voters.

"Get Up Off the Couch" happens one person at a time. I'll profile ways this can happen with the hopes of reaching a tipping point for truth, justice, and Superman's reinvented American Way.

1. Aging Gratefully: The Power of Community

Communities form one person at a time. What binds us together is sorting through our personal experiences and finding a common story.

I grew up in the suburbs of East Cheyenne, Wyoming, in the 1960s and 1970s. Those were the golden days of suburbia when the kids all hung around together, and the reason our parents knew each other was because bands of kids charged through one another's houses.

Garage doors were always open, and lots of birthday parties happened on the weekends.

Here it is 40 years later, trying to recreate my childhood neighborhood. If you're wondering about my interest in aging and cohousing, I turned 65 while living in the Silver Sage Village senior cohousing community in Boulder, Colorado.

I wrote *True Stories* through my eyes based on my good, bad, and ugly experiences in life and how those have provided me resilience, living among 30 people at SSV who started as total strangers.

SSV is a traditional community that consists of 16 condominiums. Potential owners had to wait several years and burned through millions of dollars before occupancy in 2007.

We own our private homes and have poured the cohousing secret sauce over the community by agreeing through a shared vision and list of values to maintain and operate the community and its common spaces through participation and decision-making by consensus.

Silver Sagers weed the garden, manage the Common House, and keep track of the finances while enjoying each other's company at shared meals a couple of times a week.

The SSV Homeowners Association (HOA) contracts out most of the heavy lifting jobs like snow removal and lawn mowing.

I knew I was getting old, but I didn't think it would happen this fast! As of press time, the average age of the 30 or so SSV residents is around 73 years. I'm one of the youngsters.

The "American Way" was to live in a single-family home outside the urban core when World War II ended.

After 60 years, the suburban lifestyle has evolved, with suburbanites moving back to the inner cities for various reasons, locating themselves closer to jobs and entertainment centers.

The suburban flight is also partly due to "empty nesters" whose kids are out of the house and on their own.

There's no need for one or two people to live in a massive house in the suburbs.

Regardless, households are uprooting and setting up elsewhere.

Are there new unintentional communities established with neighbors interacting and getting to know each other, or are residents staying to themselves?

The fast-moving pandemic answered that question.

COVID-19 isolated people in their homes. That made me realize, and I imagine others, how much I took face-to-face contact with people for granted.

Online Zoom rooms and Google Meet Ups kept communities engaged in two dimensions.

Interacting with someone in a little pixelated box on a computer monitor is not the same as being in the same room.

I had a lot of spare time on my hands. COVID or no COVID, I spend a lot of time writing books and editing documentary movies in front of the computer screen.

During my extra time in self-isolation, I wrote books. I self-published this book and *True Stories of a Mediocre Writer* about how I got a contract from Winter Goose Publishing that released my first memoir, *Beyond Heart Mountain,* after a 15-minute pitch in 2022.

Human-ranging patterns and balancing my life in the human and natural environments have always been interests of mine.

I studied ecological biology and environmental politics as an undergrad and grad student. I melded my majors together that resulted in a multidisciplinary approach to community development, which has been important to me since my first job in Gillette, Wyoming.

In a past life, I was a city planner at my second job in Lander, Wyoming, where the city engineer and I developed a passive solar housing subdivision for low to moderate-income owners.

Later, I served a term on the city of Boulder Planning Board in Colorado. Before that, I worked as the housing project director of Habitat for Humanity of the St. Vrain Valley in Longmont.

I've melded my academic life science, social science background, and passive interest in cost-efficient housing and am now a cohousing advocate.

That all mixes the human condition within the physical environment by creating intentional communities.

The traditional cohousing idea is a lot about the buildings where residents participate in their neighborhoods' design, character, and culture. Early on, there was less emphasis on setting up an old-fashioned sense of community.

I propose that the emphasis should be on nurturing a community of people before they get to know one another as they pick out the color of carpeting. There needs to be other topics of interest that bind the community together once the buildings are built and occupied.

There are many books on the racks about how to build cohousing and maybe about steps to find people to live in your community.

I've been on a mission to close social and economic divides and propose that intentional living in a consensus community is an excellent place to institutionalize inclusivity into the broader American society.

In the past, there was a high-level consensus about stomping out the polio epidemic. Baby Boomers, including myself, are no strangers to global pandemics.

The polio pandemic happened during World War II and peaked in the mid-1950s. There was no blaming the origins of polio on a racial or ethnic group.

Staving off polio was a big rallying point for my family. Fighting polio was very patriotic. Nobody wanted Americans to die and give the Communists an edge.

My extended close-knit family gathered at my grandparents' house in South Cheyenne, Wyoming.

Then we walked over to the fire station and waited in line to get our pink vaccine squirted onto a sugar cube.

A vigilant citizenry did its part to stomp out polio in the United States after the oral polio vaccine hit the streets in the early 1960s.

The COVID-19 pandemic was a lot different. The country became divided. There were no international foes to fight that threatened Superman's American Way.

The question asked, "Are we self-interested survivors or collaborative helpers?" America has always had divisions, generally along with these two choices. The divide became more apparent during times of social distancing and self-isolation.

Whether you thought the COVID-19 disease was a hoax, maybe no worse than the common flu, or a substantial public health problem that required high levels of vigilance, your belief wasn't important.

The world turned upside down. Old folks sneaked out of the house, and their kids yelled at them to stay indoors.

All I know is I'm an old guy who recovered from an exotic lung disease diagnosed in 2013 and part of the population vulnerable to infection of not only one of the COVID variants but any infectious disease.

In my opinion, it didn't matter if there were 200,000 or 20 million dead due to the pandemic.

I didn't want to be one of them.

COVID-19 became politicized by the 45th President. His conservative followers valued individual liberty more than the public good. Many staunchly supported the rhetoric and died on account of it.

My bottom line, people were getting sick and dying. I was overly cautious, less so now. If more of us were hyper-vigilant, there would have been fewer deaths, and the pandemic would have waned sooner.

There's nothing like a good crisis to unite communities, whether it's two neighbors dealing with a power outage during a snow blizzard or sewing masks for everyone in the neighborhood during a viral pandemic.

At least in my experience, living in cohousing isn't perfect, but the intentionality brings neighbors together to work through challenging issues. Some may be on the petty side, like, do we get rid of that old chair or not, or do we allow pet ferrets in the Common House?

They might as well be matters of life and death.

The upshot is that if there's a housing configuration suited to forcing conversations among divergent opinions, it's cohousing.

Nationally, I estimate 30,000 people live in 170 existing communities, 150 in the formative stage or just have an interest.

By definition, I think cohousers are suited to overcome social isolation, not just resulting from COVID-19 distancing, but otherwise.

We've chosen this cooperative, consensus-based lifestyle and dealt with the pandemic and other less grave issues more collaboratively.

Superman's American Way drives us to pull ourselves up by our bootstraps, make a lot of money, and be on top.

These cultural norms are roadblocks to the advancement of caring and interactive communities beyond what is familiar.

Cohousers examine their personal histories and make changes to become more inclusive instead of just believing that accepting all based on who they are is a good idea.

The American culture inhibits cohousing from entering the mainstream as it has in other countries because of rugged individualism.

Cohousing concepts are just now being understood, particularly during these times of social and physical isolation.

The popular media are starting to recognize living in cohousing communities as a mainstream lifestyle.

Stories about cohousing have been printed in the *New York Times* and aired on *National Public Radio* and local news sources.

Cohousing is the American brand for a concept brought to the United States and adapted by two architects, Katie McCamant and Chuck Durrett. In my view, cohousing was popular in Europe because the economy was flatter because the citizenry was more collaborative. More shared public services like healthcare and housing support were provided in exchange for paying higher taxes.

In the United States, cohousing was more attractive to people with accumulated or inherited wealth. The American model is a private financing mechanism that spreads around the risk among the project developer and the future owners.

Cohousing is inaccessible to most people. There is an untapped number of potential cohousers who like the idea but lack the resources to buy into a community.

I'll discuss alternative cohousing configurations that are more accessible to those with limited incomes and money and ways to develop messages to reach that market.

According to the Cohousing Research Network (CRN), the typical cohouser has a high income, a high perceived social class, is highly educated, politically progressive, Caucasian, and 70 percent of the time is a woman.

Traditional cohousing generally takes many years to build and costs millions of dollars. Even homes considered to be low-cost are not to most people.

According to the CRN, cohousers who live in retrofitted or rental communities are more likely to include racial and ethnic diversity, lower and middle perceived social class, low to moderate-income wage earners, progressives, and more single mothers.

The cohousing movement could catalyze positive change, including new ways to deal with crises, including COVID-19 and natural disasters like blizzards, tornadoes, forest fires, and tornadoes.

A trip to New York City would signal a drastic life change that ultimately led me to write this book.

An activity on my list of things to do was ride on the Cyclone roller coaster at Coney Island in New York City.

Growing up in Cheyenne, I found the roller coaster to be one of the best rides at Kiddie Land in Lions Park. The biggest thrills were a couple of banked turns.

When I was a senior at Hastings College, one of my classes was a month-long field trip to Florida called "The Ecology of the Southeast United States."

I liked to go on these out-of-state classes. The student body was small, and I met kids I wouldn't normally associate, like football players from the "jock dorm."

We lived in cabins in the Bahia Honda State Park camp on Big Pine Key. Because it was a class, a prescribed schedule, and social structure revolved around preparing and sharing common meals.

There were planned field trips. We created strong social bonds by working as individuals and in teams.

One of the stops was at Disney World. It was still relatively new, opening in 1971 when I graduated from high school.

At that time, the waiting lines were still manageable, and I could ride Space Mountain, which was a thrill because the ride took place in the dark, and there was no frame of reference.

That was my biggest roller coaster ride until I made it to Coney Island in June 2013.

I traveled with my partner, Diana, who was on her way to visit her family in Boston.

We stayed over with my college Eta Phi Lambda fraternity brother, Tom. He's lived in the same rent-controlled apartment on the Upper Westside on 72nd Street since we've been out of college.

His place is a few blocks from Central Park and the Dakota apartment building where John Lennon was gunned down.

The Cyclone was a definite thrill ride. After getting back to the bottom, I needed two Nathan's hot dogs after my dizziness subsided.

While on the Cyclone, I received a phone call from a movie director named Joe.

After getting off the ride, I called back. Joe asked if I could help with some production services for his project *Mahjong and the West* (2015), which I agreed to do.

That night, I woke up in the middle of the night with a sharp pain pinpointed on the left side of my scalp.

Upon my return, I had a big road trip scheduled around Wyoming, interviewing artists awarded fellowships from the Wyoming Arts Council.

The next day, I made the long drive to Northwest Wyoming. After stops in Jackson and Cody, my face and scalp broke out with small Shingles sores.

It was downhill from there after a trip to an urgent care clinic.

My drive around Wyoming took a toll on me. I became lethargic, had difficulty breathing, and lost a lot of weight.

Compounding it all, I became involved in the *Mahjong and the West* production in Jackson.

As it turned out, commuting from Boulder to Jackson was a massive mistake, as the stress exacerbated my illness.

I ended up handling much of the production work from Colorado.

A little later in the summer, I was still getting sicker when my Cheyenne friends Bob and Jill asked me to document the wedding of their daughter, Jessica, and her fiancée, Eddie.

After the blessed event, I ended up in the hospital for a week, where I mainlined steroids.

Overworked, I was rested after the hospital stay. In the long run, I didn't get any better.

Fast forward to mid-December 2013. One night, I was so sick that Diana drove me to Good Samaritan Hospital, 20 miles away in Lafayette, and dropped me off. She went back to Boulder to pack me a bag.

The thought was that the hospital would admit me that night. I went through triage in the Emergency Room (ER) but was released.

My across-the-sidewalk neighbor, Jim, drove to the hospital to bring me back to SSV.

A day later, December 15th, was the SSV community holiday party after the Sunday potluck dinner. The fare was my favorite - turkey and roast beef with all the fixings, but none was appetizing, and I barely touched my plate.

I went home after dinner and missed the white elephant gift exchange. The next day, I sprawled out on the couch.

Diana called 911. Cops, a fire truck, and an ambulance all pulled up with lights flashing. The ambulance hauled me back to the hospital.

The check-in desk immediately admitted me into the Intensive Care Unit (ICU).

These days, there's lots of talk about COVID-19 patients having difficulty breathing. As soon as I hit the ICU bed, it was a big relief, even though I couldn't breathe.

The ICU nurse outfitted me with a regular respirator, but it didn't force enough air into my lungs. I wasn't sick enough to have a ventilator tube stuck down my windpipe.

The ICU nurse strapped some sort of attachment on my face that blew more air into my nose. I can sleep through just about anything, but that was noisy.

When I moved into the SSV senior cohousing community, I understood the cohousing concept intellectually. About all I knew was there were many meetings by committees managing various aspects of community life. Having a past life as a bureaucrat, I could handle those.

After landing in the hospital ICU, my hubris concealed my illness since I had so many irons in the fire that needed to be pounded out during January and February 2014.

There's no way I wanted to expose that I needed help.

Being the eternal optimist, I figured to be back in the office by Christmas.

Nonetheless, word got out, and some friends, neighbors, and colleagues stopped to visit.

Following my admission to the hospital, my health hadn't improved much. Christmas came and went. I was still flat on my back.

Since my parents died in 2003, celebrating the winter holidays has been different every year.

Being in a hospital for Christmas with the second-tier staff on duty would be the most different Christmas of my life, but not surprising.

"How did you end up working on a big holiday?" I asked whoever was in the room at the moment.

"My kids are with their mother this year, and I work on Christmas. We celebrated last week, so I got a good dose of the festivities," would be a typical response. "Plus, I get paid more."

I also built strong relationships with the hospital caregivers and tipped my hat to healthcare workers in the trenches, namely nurses and certified nurse assistants (CNAs).

The healthcare world wouldn't turn without them. I'll jump ahead and say that I'd never had a lengthy hospital stay before.

After laying flat on my back for six weeks, the extended stay convinced me that the hospital's primary function is to keep patients alive, not necessarily to get them better.

I couldn't walk or stand up, and it was excruciatingly painful when I tried. I developed bedsores and couldn't wipe my butt.

Luckily, nurses and CNAs were there to meet my every need, particularly when I felt bummed out.

One night, I dreamt of suddenly standing up and getting around in a walker.

The room was sideways, like inside the Space Shuttle, where I climbed around on the walls using hand holds. I woke up terrified in a room by myself.

I kept pushing the call button, but nobody came. It was a very helpless feeling.

A nurse finally showed up, and I yelled at her for not being at her post, which was a big overreaction.

I expected a certain level of service unavailable in the middle of the night.

That lack of support from the hospital staff raises another big topic: self-advocacy.

I was complacent, mostly because I was mentally and physically out of it and couldn't advocate for myself as much as I should have.

If you end up as bad off as me, persuade a couple of your friends to advocate for you. It's a thankless, time-consuming, and mentally draining job.

Diana was a big advocate. She questioned and kept on the nurses and doctors.

She brought over one of our SSV neighbors and another friend with experience advocating for hospital patients.

They provided significant bits of help, particularly early in my stay. I can't say enough about having strong advocates.

My pulmonologist, Dr. Kinnard, became my newest best friend during this time. What happened next is a bit of a blur.

Dr. Kinnard had several biopsies done on my chest using Video-Assisted Thoracoscopic Surgery (VATS) to figure out what might be causing my mysterious pneumonia.

The VATS is minimally invasive and resulted in a bunch of holes punched into my lungs. That was another painful experience.

Fluids accumulated around all the wounds and drained into a bucket beside my bed.

Did I mention the morphine pump?

Meanwhile, I was on steroids, which, in part, led to a duodenal ulcer that perforated the small intestine near my stomach. Septic contents were leaking into my body cavity.

I didn't have an appetite. The nurses kept trying to force Jell-O and apple sauce down my trap.

I don't know this as a fact, but I was told later that following the biopsies, doctors didn't give me much of a chance to make it through the emergency surgery to patch up the ulcer.

Having no appetite and general mental indifference translated into "failure to thrive."

The CNAs left some tiny sponges stuck onto sticks like a lollipop. I dipped them in water to moisten my mouth.

I was reminded of a scene from one of those "Bible" movies. One of His advocates dipped a wad of fabric stuck on a wooden rod into a bucket of water. Then it was raised, and Jesus quenched his thirst by sucking out the moisture.

The sponges are offered to patients on their last legs. I'm glad nobody mentioned that to me at the time.

After the emergency ulcer surgery, I was fed yellow gunky pablum through a Peripherally Inserted Central Catheter (PICC) line tube, bypassing my stomach and intestines while the ulcer patch healed.

The PICC diet caused me to lose weight and strength. When I later reviewed my medical record, the doctor classified me as anorexic.

After losing 37 pounds, I dropped to 107, which was how much I weighed in high school.

A laboratory at the University of Michigan sent back the lung biopsy results that figured out my lung condition was autoimmune pneumonia called Pneumocystis Pneumonia (PCP).

Go Wolverines! I rooted for Michigan to win the NCAA National Championship in 2024.

PCP is the same disease that killed AIDS patients with compromised immune systems in the 1980s.

After New Year's Day, it was clear the hospital was pretty much done with me, and I was kicked out and sent to a rehab center in Denver.

While I wouldn't trade my stint in the ICU for anything, what I learned about myself was life-changing, but I don't recommend it as the best way to lose weight.

I didn't get what living in an intentional community was about emotionally until I was on my deathbed in December 2013 and, like Ebenezer Scrooge, visited by the Ghost of Christmases Yet to Come.

Think back about your past living experiences growing up and where you've lived over the years.

Those memories will give insight into how you might fit into a cohousing community.

For me, my life-long experiences set me up to live in cohousing.

I decided to Get Up Off the Couch and SHARE this message about the power of community.

2. Cohousing Evolution Revolution

I'll define "cohousing" and its various frameworks and explain why collaborative housing can add less expensive options to the housing mix.

It's common knowledge that a shortage of lower-cost housing across the country affects low and moderate-income households.

If the cohousing definition changes, it could be one of the solutions. A cohousing community is currently defined as one that includes residents who live in private homes. That means those that have private bathrooms and kitchens.

As discussed later, I'll make a case that the definition should be changed to "private dwellings" with an access door that can be locked.

According to the U.S. Department of Urban Development (HUD), housing costs have outpaced income.

Low-income households are the most vulnerable, but middle-income families have also felt the effects of this trend.

Middle-class families generally don't have a problem paying the recommended 30 percent of their income on housing.

Families with children, especially families with children in the lowest middle-class income bracket, face overcrowding as households with more than two people per bedroom.

If developers and investors could make money building bargain-basement-priced housing, there would be no shortage.

Some estimates say that up to two-thirds of renters across the nation say they can't afford to buy a home.

Since home prices are rising at a rate twice that of wage growth, saving up for that down payment is a more significant challenge.

Millennials and GenXers with high student debt are in this boat, as are some older folks who, for one reason or another, weren't able to build any extra savings.

High-density communities like cohousing are one way to provide inexpensive housing to owners and renters.

The private home cohousing model originated in Denmark during the 1960s. Architects Katie McCamant and Chuck Durrett brought the concept to the United States in the 1980s.

The social and cultural challenge is adapting community-building tenets into the "rugged individualistic" lifestyle of Superman's American Way.

There are 10,000 Baby Boomers who turn 65 every day. This trend is expected to last through at least the next decade.

A housing shortage is predicted as the Baby Boomer population expands and ages.

If you can't afford to buy a home or your rent is too high, how can cohousing meet your needs?

Housing is housing, and what differentiates cohousing from other configurations is the "secret sauce," which I'll later share in more depth.

The Typical Cohouser: The traditional cohousing model has evolved over the years, but the basic tenets remain constant. There's a version of cohousing for everyone.

I live in Boulder, Colorado, where microbreweries are part of the economic base. I categorize cohousing communities as three types of beer.

Data from a 2012 CRN study by Angela Sanguinetti compared retrofit cohousing community residents (those that grow into residential developments) with traditional cohousing community residents (new-build or adapted developments that start from scratch).

Cohousing Beer: Boulder is a microbrew beer town. I classify cohousing communities into three beer types. According to the CRN, there are differences among the residents who live in the various configurations:

Coho Ultra-Lite: The CRN study found that retrofit Coho Ultra-Lite residents did not differ from Coho Stout and Lite residents in terms of political affiliation or education level but were more racially diverse, liberal, middle-class, moderate-income, more singles, and single parents.

Ultra-Lite residents live in "private dwellings," generally a room with a door that locks. They share a kitchen and bathrooms.

Like in most cohousing communities, a few "burning souls" who are highly engaged and interested in cohousing envision transforming an existing neighborhood, repurposing a building, or building a community among members who don't live in the same location.

Ultra-Lite may mitigate some barriers for a broader group of interested cohousers by being less resource-intensive.

Ultra-Lite is the most cost-effective and quickest approach, allowing for more rental options.

During development, architects and real estate professionals generally play supportive roles.

Ultra-Lite can also be a community of people who don't live in the same proximity.

The cohousing culture is what makes the community. One such group is Beacon Hill Village.

It's an existing dispersed community of 500 seniors who agree upon how to be active and supportive of one another rather than reliant on others to "take care" of them all the time.

The community members provide neighborly support to one another by coordinating outside social activities and providing physical caregiving.

The Beacon Hill Village approach would be appropriate for multigenerational communities as well.

Since all are aging, it seems like people don't get around to planning for their life care until it's almost too late.

A guy I know named Greg formed Boulder Creek Cohousing. He purchased several condominiums and embedded the cohousing community within the larger Gold Run HOA.

Resident turnover is discouraged because the community deposits a portion of each month's rent in a limited-equity escrow account.

The set-aside amount is paid back to the tenant upon departure.

Boulder Creek Cohousing doesn't worry about fixing the roof or painting the building since the master HOA board makes those decisions.

The community's "higher purpose" is one of service. The group spends more time strengthening its membership.

In one case, the master HOA provided funds for materials, and the cohousing community improved a part of the shared open space.

There also is "accidental cohousing," as is the case of the CBS TV show *Big Bang Theory* (2007 - 2019).

The elevator has been out for years in the apartment house where Sheldon, Amy, Leonard, Penny, Howard, and Bernadette live.

The TV characters use the stairway as a common area where they have conversations every show. They rotate around the various apartments and share meals.

Their decisions are made by consensus, with the many often having to compromise towards Sheldon's minority position.

In one episode, the group acquired a dining room table set.

All sat around enjoying their meal while Sheldon didn't give up their tradition of sitting around the coffee table.

The others decided to join Sheldon at their usual seats on the couch and floor.

In real life, the Canyon Pointe senior citizen apartment complex in Downtown Boulder, Colorado, is an accidental community that naturally occurred among tenants.

A resident council organizes activities and advises Boulder Housing Partners, the local housing authority that owns and manages the property.

On each floor, residents know their neighbors, watch out for irregularities, and provide neighborly support for one another.

They share common outdoor gardens. Residents share dinners, holidays, and other celebrations in a newly refurbished community room.

Coho Stout and Coho Lite: Caucasian, liberal, high perceived social class, high income, high education level, 70 percent of the time a woman. The CRN study found that people interested in Coho Stout and Lite must also have the time to wait and money to build. At the same time, the project manager processes the development through local government planning, zoning, and building offices.

Coho Stout and Lite's residents live in private houses with bathrooms and kitchens.

A Lite developer, along with design and real estate professionals, drives the project. The community burning souls may or may not be out recruiting members.

Coho Lite is less capital-intensive for future residents since the developer is responsible for buying the land, hiring the architect, and building the houses.

The homeowners only have to obtain financing for their houses.

Because the community members don't have to go through land acquisition, select design professionals, or process the project through the local government planning and zoning maze, more time can be devoted to establishing the community.

An example is **Bloomington Cohousing** in Indiana. The developer, named Loren, is financing and constructing the project designed by an architect who worked with the burning souls to envision some basic floor plans.

Loren built a model home, which is typical of traditional housing developments. The community is being organized concurrently but separately from the project development.

The shared picnic area is complete. As the developer builds the homes, the future residents gather there during nice weather.

Another example is Genesee Garden in Lansing, Michigan, which was formed in 2003.

The neighbors transformed an existing area rather than building from the ground up.

Residents removed the back fences to create a large common area, the Genesee Garden.

The community formed an HOA and acquired nearby homes when they became available for purchase. The HOA converted one of the 10 houses into the Common House.

My friend and colleague, Ty, is developing a hybrid project between Lite and Ultra-Lite called the East Bluff Backyard Community Neighborhood in Sulphur Springs, Oklahoma.

He and his partner subdivided a piece of land into eight detached single-family houses.

Each home is built one at a time with "sweat equity," meaning the two developers aren't paying themself. Materials and supplies are purchased from their savings to avoid debt financing.

They are waiting until the end to net a profit.

The project is cohousing in reverse. The community forms organically. The eight houses back up to a 50 ft backyard easement. Owners agree through deed restriction that they will maintain the space.

Within that easement is a common area that includes the mailboxes and other uses agreed upon by the community, like gardens and picnic areas.

The Coho Stout variety is the traditional community structure. Burning souls build partnerships with an architect and other real estate professionals.

Projects are very capital intensive, with the developers and future community members sharing the entire development risk.

Potential residents who want to live together must also have the financial resources to invest in land, design, and construction, the patience to decide on the paint color, landscaping, and the time to wait while all this happens.

Where I live, SSV is a Coho Stout community with 16 condominiums that tend toward the demographic extremes.

Boulder Housing Partners owned the former Holiday drive-in movie theater and parceled out the property into small pieces.

It was a high-density housing laboratory.

The city of Boulder heavily subsidized the entire Holiday Neighborhood to encourage socioeconomic diversity, with 40 percent of the homes reserved for residents who met the city's lower-priced housing program criteria.

The SSV community has six lower-priced, deed-restricted houses that are 800 sq ft.

Contrast those with 10 homes that are "market rate" and range in size from 1,000 to 3,000 sq ft.

Not only are the large condos triple in size, but also triple in cost.

While income diversity may seem like a good thing, households that can afford to pay a million bucks for a home have a different worldview than those who live in a $200,000 place.

There are different views about the value of money and standards of living.

Traditional Coho Stout can't be built quickly or inexpensively enough to meet the growing demand, particularly for the aging population.

This ground-up process often takes three to five years or more, with potential members coming and going and more accessible to people and families with inherited wealth or adequate disposable savings.

These three beer categories are broad. Any community can permutate the descriptions and change them to meet their needs.

2a. Tiny House Cohousing

On a recent quick trip to Estes Park, there's a place to stay in Lyon's Colorado called **Wee Casa**.

It's a tiny house resort laid out like an RV park with a community room. Each house is available to rent for the night or an extended stay.

When it comes to efficiently-priced housing, tiny houses are invariably mentioned in the context of low-cost tiny house cohousing.

It's a hybrid of all three cohousing microbrew types - zombie beer.

There's been talk about low-cost housing types for Millennials paying off student debt, seniors seeking less expensive independent living alternatives, and marginalized populations like veterans experiencing homelessness.

Tiny houses are low-cost to construct. A tiny house burning soul could cram many onto a piece of ground.

As such, some city governments are building small homes for those in need of housing options.

A tiny house community makes some sense, but its development has more challenges than appears on the surface.

Tiny houses epitomize the Reinvented American Way in which smaller is better than larger, and less is better than more.

Over the past few years, interest among people choosing to live in 200 to 400-sq ft homes has grown.

Tiny houses cost anywhere from $20,000 to $60,000 with a combination of cash and sweat equity.

Owners can park them in friends' backyards as accessory dwelling units (ADU).

Tiny houses are generally constructed on a flatbed trailer frame that the owner can wheel around from place to place or permanently built on a foundation.

Permanence kicks in an entirely different set of building requirements.

Tiny houses on skids or wheels fall into the land-use category of mobile homes or temporary housing.

An ADU is technical jargon that generally encompasses backyard sheds and playhouses but is interpreted to include tiny houses.

Tiny houses are far different from your typical mobile home.

Regular mobile homes can be the size of stick-built places that incorporate some space-saving design features.

State and local governments impose mobile home design standards. The mobile home industry is a strong lobbying group.

If too popular, tiny houses infringe on the mobile home industry monopoly.

If you google "tiny house," many websites and images pop up. There are several cable TV shows dedicated to the topic.

The host/developer and an innovative builder work with people, mostly downsizing Baby Boomers, young couples, and individuals making moves to drop out of the "bigger is better" society.

Tiny houses are very customized. The TV episodes include the challenges of space-saving innovations to meet the owners' particular needs, like extra space to store outdoor gear or places to play music.

The biggest hurdles for tiny house developments, traditional cohousing, and regular housing, for that matter, are government regulations and money.

From a zoning code standpoint, tiny house communities will likely be a land use without a zoning designation.

Work with your local planning and zoning official and creatively determine how tiny houses fit into their regulations.

Money to buy land and pay development costs is also a typical impediment.

Because cost is such a factor, like all housing developments, cohousing developers construct houses to maximize profit by sprinkling in some expensive homes.

"Income diversity" is advertised as a good thing when selling a cohousing development. That's a double-edged sword, which I'll discuss later.

How about the opposite model, inexpensive houses crammed onto tiny spaces that result in more open space?

The tiny house community will likely be more transient because some owners want to be more mobile, and others may choose to be long-term, permanent residents.

A tiny house community is likely to be a commercial venture instead of a residential one, may fall under a different set of regulations, and may be more expensive.

The development may best fit into a developer-driven Coho Lite project.

I heard an idea based in the Pacific Northwest about a cohousing community wondering about peeling off a piece of its property for a tiny house village.

At some point, figuring out how to manage the place will be necessary. Without a good number of long-term residents, decision-making would be very diffuse.

It could be a subdivision with private lots sold. Some may be rentals owned by the community, like Wee Casa.

Is a tiny house a mobile home? Maybe it's an ADU? How do the uniform building codes apply?

Utilities could be "hook-ups," like in an RV park. Depending on the political jurisdiction, a developer's decision about public utilities would need to be made.

Options may include choices between individual septic and water cisterns, an HOA-managed septic field, a private central water system, or local government-provided water distribution and wastewater collection.

A tiny house community would include amenities like streets, sidewalks, and open space in addition to the Common House.

At a typical RV park, the longer-stay "residents" have access to the shared showers/restrooms, laundry, the convenience store, and breakfast available to the overnight campers.

I can envision a Common House that is more permanent as a monetary hedge against potentially higher turnover rates. Like at a KOA campground, it could be mixed uses.

A separate business that contracts with the HOA or the HOA could operate and manage the community amenities like a convenience store, coffee shop, an open dining area, kitchen, laundry facilities, TV room, guest rooms, and other offices.

Because tiny houses are small, residents would be more likely to frequent the Common House.

Compare that to large homes in Coho Stout communities with large living rooms, utility rooms, and big kitchens.

At SSV, there are several houses over 3,000 square feet in size. They are houses taken from a suburban neighborhood and dropped into a condo community.

Like in the suburbs, some of my neighbors go into their houses, and you don't see them again. My office is in the Common House. I won't hear or see anyone except when they come to check their mail. My observation is that the primary Common House users live in the small condos.

Formal dining areas, dens, and large kitchens are unfounded housing characteristics necessary for resale, as espoused by Sarah Susanka, who wrote *Not So Big House* (1998).

"How many of you have a formal dining room in your house," she asked during a presentation at the University of Denver, where I heard her speak. Much of the audience raised their hands.

"How many of you use your formal dining room?" Hardly anyone raised their hands.

She talked about the misconceptions about housing prices and desired amenities.

Historically, houses have specific characteristics like dens and dining rooms that are designed into places but end up underutilized spaces.

Her idea is to design more functional homes that meet the needs of households. The quality of the space is more important than quantity.

Coho Lite developments have fewer customizations. The cohousing-savvy developer would offer efficient floor plans to encourage residents to frequent the Common House.

I'd say that, for the most part, cities still have a bias AGAINST mobile home parks and hold the "trailer trash" stereotype.

In a place like Boulder, there would be an uproar about this as a form of low-cost, newly constructed housing.

The best place to try this out would be where land is inexpensive and there is less of an elitist attitude.

Housing people experiencing homelessness has received the most traction for tiny house communities.

Denver has a self-governed **tiny house village called** "Beloved" for people without housing. When it opened, there were 11 residences and a Common House.

The Beloved community had a six-month temporary zoning permit for the current location and later moved the entire village.

There's a social stigma around housing for those experiencing homelessness. Local mainstream cultures should be open to tiny houses for "regular" people.

If the concept works here, why not in another setting? Wee Casa figured it out.

2b. Commercial Retrofits

The main beef I hear about cohousing is about the price of the homes. I've been talking to anyone who'll listen to me about lowering cohousing costs through **retrofit options**.

One idea out there is about repurposing vacant big-box retail stores and abandoned shopping malls into lower-cost, high-density housing.

Conventional wisdom says it's cheaper to scrape off the big box and build new ones.

I envision the cohousing secret sauce poured over small dwelling units with access to shared facilities like kitchen and dining areas, shared baths, and shared living spaces.

Think of a condominium complex of tiny houses with shared walls.

A selling point would be small interior footprints tricked out with tiny house-like space-saving gadgetry like drawers under stairs or a table that, when flipped over, exposes a TV monitor.

The retrofit idea was straightforward until the COVID-19 pandemic put up the biggest obstacle.

Designing for social distancing is a critical challenge to overcome.

Almost by definition, the market predicates cost-efficient and lower-priced housing on high density. People in close quarters means a higher risk of disease transmission.

I happened to have a facebook conversation with a colleague named Delia. I hadn't been in touch with her for many years. She reminded me that I interviewed her for a series of social justice videos.

I mentioned to her my interest in converting an abandoned big box store into lower-priced cohousing.

"Why not Colorado Springs?" she responded. "I have a similar idea."

Plenty of vacant buildings around the country, including Colorado Springs, are sitting empty.

Commercial buildings of all sizes are becoming obsolete in favor of online retail and pop-up stores.

The COVID-19 lockdowns are likely to force even more storefronts out of business.

I was in Portland, Oregon, for the Cohousing Association of the U.S. (CohoUS) annual conference. The burgeoning population of people experiencing homelessness was a hot local topic.

Similarly, there are health and safety concerns about campers squatted in Boulder residential areas.

While unhoused people are a population in need of better housing options, my more general concept is to apply the cohousing secret sauce to cooperative rental housing and owner-occupied cohousing.

Many grants are available to meet the needs of very low or no-income people. People with low to moderate incomes fall through the cracks.

People may work multiple jobs or otherwise have financial difficulties, are housing distressed, and cannot find a stable and safe place to live.

The most well-known shopping mall retrofit is the **Arcade Providence**, now apartments in Providence, Rhode Island.

The Aria cohousing community retrofitted an old convent in Denver.

A retrofit housing project would fit any community with a vacant big-box store, out-of-business hotels, or abandoned shopping mall.

Some places are better suited for a pilot project than others. Thousands of big-box stores are currently for sale or lease around the country.

Nationally, there are **9,300 big box stores** slated to close in 2019. That number will likely grow as a result of COVID-19 store closures.

The ideal pilot project would include a property, fallow for many years, an owner willing to be an equity partner, and cash out at the end.

During COVID-19, attracting new business to vacant storefronts was a non-starter.

People on the financial margin are getting kicked out of rental housing and could use more housing choices that are easier on their pocketbooks.

Adding more residents to a quiet commercial area provides vibrancy from more customers frequenting existing businesses like food stores, coffee shops, and other retail establishments.

A city or town with an existing cohousing community may be more open to the intentional community concept.

Colorado Springs fits that bill with the Casa Verde cohousing community located there.

Flexible Zoning: Local governments with wider open zoning and land use regulations that allow mixed uses by right or are silent on mixed-use development may be more inclined to accept retrofit housing developments.

The city of Colorado Springs and the business community are discussing the potential benefits of up-zoning the city code.

Allowing more flexibility will create more mixed-use opportunities in commercial districts, including lower-cost housing options.

Burning Souls: There should be at least one advocate interested in the project. That would be my friend, Delia, who garnered the ear of the city of Colorado Springs Community Development Office, several city council members, and now myself.

A local realtor identified three potential sites for the project.

Other helpful resources would be from the local housing authority and other housing advocates.

2c. Governance

SSV governance is based on shared responsibility, rotated leadership, and community norms about accountability.

Those are significant departures from majority rule and top-down decision-making.

An entire industry has cropped up around consensus processes, cultural competency, and meeting facilitation.

Regardless of the form of governance you select, most states have laws that define how HOAs are organized and govern their members.

Familiarize yourself with the flavors of cohousing beer. Maybe you prefer one that's more bitter or stout. Pick what you like based on your taste.

You may not want to guzzle down your brewski but rather sip slowly and think about how you want to organize and govern yourselves.

Cohousing communities generally fit within some sort of corporate structure. If you choose Coho Stout, your partnering developer may have ideas about that.

You'll likely be more interested in how your community is formally organized in a Lite community.

If you're retrofitting an existing building or happy to be a Coho Ultra-Lite community that doesn't live together, contact a similar community and find out how they got started.

Even if you're in the early stages of community formation, I suggest you organize your group in some way.

It's probably not a formal corporate structure, but at least come up with a name and maybe set up a bank account.

As you form your community, you might have a monthly membership fee, so members have skin in the game.

Those funds would be for incidental costs like advertising events, buying snacks for get-togethers, or renting meeting spaces.

As you get down the road, check out your state's laws about HOAs.

The HOA declarations are the "constitution" of the community. The organizing documents are stable, static, and establish, usually based on state law, your community rules, and norms around the conduct of meetings, the decision-making process, and resident behavior.

Specific issues, like pet policies, smoking prohibition, participation, etc., are further regulated by policies and procedures adopted by the community.

Cohousing communities don't fit the typical HOA model.

Rather than electing a board of directors to handle the HOA business, all the owners in a cohousing community generally make all the HOA decisions. Most state laws require a board of directors.

My place, SSV, is a community of teams rather than individuals.

A resident can place an issue or topic on the community agenda in two ways. We have an "initiative" process when at least four households agree to bring a topic to the community.

Otherwise, a resident can refer the issue to the appropriate team that makes recommendations to the Steering Team that prepares topics for community discussion, consideration, and approval.

The Steering Team derives its authority from the community and ratifies any decisions made following the monthly general community meeting.

I receive emails from community burning souls requesting copies of HOA documents or templates on the cohousing social media pages.

I don't think there's a shortcut to this step.

Your first stop should be the state agency that regulates HOAs. Each state will have a page with frequently asked questions and likely some downloadable sample documents specific to that state.

HOAs are highly regulated because a few traditional HOA boards were rife with problems like insider business dealings, loans made to board members, contractor favoritism, and outright theft.

If traditional HOAs governed themselves like cohousing HOAs in which all owners have a say, there would be fewer problems around transparency and accountability.

When you get your hands on a copy of the state's HOA regulations, then the tweaking step begins.

Unless you're a process wonk or someone with government experience implementing rules and regulations, you may be frustrated conforming cohousing to the state requirements.

I was on the Finance and Legal Team, which revised the SSV declarations. The task was to cohousing-ize the language.

For example, that team adapted language around Parliamentary Procedure to reflect consensus decision-making.

Colorado state law calls out supermajorities and simple majorities. That jargon doesn't apply in consensus decision-making.

Consensus approval requires 100 percent consent, meaning the "majority rule" thresholds are always met.

The housing development process is an institution that's been in place since President Franklin Roosevelt pushed his New Deal during the Great Depression in the 1930s.

The COVID-19 pandemic brought to light glaring social and economic disparities among Americans and why access to safe and cost-efficient housing should be a fundamental right.

Lower-cost cohousing is one answer to relieve housing insecurity.

I'd say lack of time and money are the main reasons the lower-cost housing industrial complex hasn't made many strides other than to tweak the existing system.

Maybe my provoking discussion as a result of this book will increase the chance of social change happening.

3. Taste the Secret Sauce and SHARE

As a kid, I had a big, close-knit extended family. I wasn't a stranger to close quarters and living on top of others.

I'd say that four phases in my life shaped my affinity for cohousing.

When I was young, I first poured the intentional community secret sauce over my housing situations.

That experience set me up for my other living situations I chose as an adult. The cohousing secret sauce has certain essential ingredients:

• **Socialize:** Get to know your community members. If we hope to build stronger relationships, we have to get out there and meet our neighbors.

• **Help Out:** Lend a hand. Not only should we be charitable during the holiday giving season at the end of each year, but what about the other 50 calendar weeks?

• **Accept:** Include others without judgment. Making decisions about someone based on inaccurate or incomplete information defines stereotyping. How did the way you grew up help determine how you view people who may be different from yourself today?

• **Reach Out:** Meet people, unlike yourself, with respect and dignity. How can we break out of our comfort zone?

• **Engage:** Help save the world by doing good, doing no harm, and being friendly. How do we set aside differences and bridge cultural and social divides?

Big Family – Cheyenne, Wyoming: I tasted my first spoonful of the secret sauce growing up in the 1950s and 1960s with a big extended family.

Those early experiences set the table for future living arrangements that eventually ended in a cohousing community.

Both sets of grandparents and numerous uncles, aunts, and cousins all lived in Cheyenne.

Cheyenne was the central gathering point during the summer and holidays when both sets of grandparents were living.

One summer, I had to give up my room to my grandfather, who stayed with us when my grandmother didn't have time to provide care.

She was the cook at the family business, the Highway Café. Plus, all my other aunts and uncles worked.

My mother was a stay-at-home mom and had time to devote to my grandfather's primary caregiving responsibilities.

Dad moved my bedroom to the living room couch. That was good for me because it was near the TV.

I visited my grandfather each morning to check on him and my room. He was laid up with diabetes and couldn't see too well out of one eye.

Each morning, he had to jab himself with insulin.

Back then, he injected his medicine using a big stainless-steel needle stuck onto the end of a Pyrex glass barrel and pushed into his muscle with a giant plunger.

There were no disposable hypodermic needles back then. Grandfather taught me how to administer his shot.

To this day, I'm not fearful of needles. Before COVID-19, I underwent acupuncture treatments once or twice a week until the clinic closed.

Not only was my extended family an intentional community, but also the neighborhood where I grew up.

I was in the first grade, and my sister was a year away from kindergarten. My parents moved into the Cole Addition, a suburb of Cheyenne that sprung up after World War II and during the Cold War.

Cheyenne was soon home to the country's highest density of nuclear missiles.

Besides, the school district changed boundaries in anticipation of the impending growth. Had we not moved, I would have had to leave Fairview Elementary to attend a different school my mom thought was on the seedy side.

We moved three blocks away from Fairview. Our new Cole Addition suburban-like neighborhood was primarily young families.

Because the kids knew each other, all our parents got to know each other. Garage doors were always open, and packs of us would gather at each other's homes.

We all palled around during the school year and also during the summer. The community swimming pools were the gathering points.

The three major suburbs - Cole Addition, Buffalo Ridge, and Sun Valley, all had community pools, which were big draws.

The Cole pool was within walking distance for every kid. We took tennis lessons and had moonlight swimming parties.

The pools all had a swim team that competed. I was a lousy swimmer and watched those from poolside.

When I graduated from Cheyenne East High School, a group of my Presbyterian Church friends and I decided we would attend Hastings College in Hastings, Nebraska.

Even though we all lived in different parts of town and attended other schools, we became friends from camp in the summer and hung out at the church's youth fellowship club on Sunday afternoons.

Thinking back, I realized my childhood memories were all pleasant ones. My family was living the stereotypical American Way.

Like in a cohousing community, each family lived in their own homes and lived separate lives.

We all were bound together by our shared experiences and participated in formal and informal neighborhood activities and events.

Altman Hall Dorm Rat – Hastings, Nebraska: I was an Altman Hall homebody at Hastings College.

Room 101 was at the end of the hall next to the telephone, the exit door, and the stairway to the basement, where the recreation room, laundry, and kitchen were located.

It was very convenient. So convenient, I stayed in the same room for four years. My classmates wanted to flee campus living as quickly as they could.

As for myself, I enjoyed sitting in the cafeteria with my classmates.

On Wednesdays, the dinner was family-style. We had to find six dinnermates and dress up.

The formal dinner social engineering drill taught me not to use my salad fork throughout the entire meal. Plus, I didn't have to cook.

The food service was called SAGA, "A GAS spelled backward." The fare was "all you can eat."

That included endless hamburgers and desserts. I gained 30 pounds before my first Fall Break.

One of my favorite dishes at college was Chili Fritos.

It was a plate of shredded iceberg lettuce covered with a bed of Fritos corn chips and smothered with chili. That's a comfort food that I prepare today.

The Five and Dime department store on the Central Plaza in Santa Fe, New Mexico, sells a similar dish called Frito Pie at its snack counter.

Besides taking my tray to the back, I didn't have to load the dishwasher and stack them after they were clean and dry.

It was paradise since clearing the table and washing dishes were household chores at home.

I liked lingering afterward, shooting pool, or playing ping pong in Bellevue House, the student union.

Altman Hall was the co-ed dorm with men on one side and women on the opposite side, joined by the shared basement where there was also the TV room. Upstairs was a common lobby.

The basement door that separated the men's and women's sides wasn't locked. There was unchecked after-hours socializing. We, "Altman Angels," had a code of silence.

The building layout led to plenty of social interaction. It was an intentional community before there was such a thing.

All the dorms, including Altman, were organized by a council selected by the residents. Our dorm council was the central point of contact for the college administration, as well as organized dorm activities.

Most kids attending Hastings were Nebraska locals who didn't stray far from home. Student lore characterized Hastings as a "suitcase college."

Some left campus on the weekends and took laundry to their parent's place.

First-year women weren't allowed to leave campus at the beginning of the first semester. I don't know why that was a gender-specific rule.

Others couldn't wait to get out of the dorms. I understood why they wanted to live off-campus as a show of independence.

I liberated myself from Wyoming, a day's drive away.

To me, that was freedom.

My family didn't expect me to travel home for birthday parties.

I made it back to Cheyenne for two out of four Fall Breaks. Since then, Thanksgiving has been a second-rate holiday for me.

After I graduated during the post-Watergate era and after the Vietnam War ended, the unemployment rate was over eight percent.

My degrees were in political science (political systems theory) and biology (environmental science), and they were not exactly the best backgrounds to find work.

There were few jobs for recent graduates, and no work was available identifying mammal teeth or analyzing whether the federation or confederation was the best form of government.

I ended up melding my political science and biology undergraduate majors into an early version of environmental politics that became the basis for my multidisciplinary view of the world, eventually leading me to cohousing.

I didn't have the faintest idea of what job I was best suited and ended up applying to graduate schools and lucked out.

At the last minute, I landed a teaching assistantship at the University of Wyoming in Laramie and ended up living with my parents for a couple of years.

They appreciated me being around, but having an extra adult in the house wasn't the same as when I was a little kid, especially when my cousin and I came back drunk one night.

3003 Club – Gillette, Wyoming: I took classes that had internships, which gave me a little more direction. The city of Gillette hired me to be a grant writer, which turned out to be my superpower.

While in Gillette, my first home ownership experience was chipping in with a couple of guys. It was an early version of a cooperative house.

A friend named Tom was a Vietnam veteran. He just graduated from law school. Tom, his friend Phil, and I chipped in and bought a home using Tom's military veteran benefits.

President Franklin Roosevelt signed the Servicemen's Readjustment Act of 1944 (G.I. Bill) after a bipartisan effort led by the American Legion.

The G.I. Bill created various programs as transitions from wartime to peacetime, including grants for college and additional hospitals.

The law also established low-interest, zero-down-payment home loans for service members, with better terms for new construction than for existing home purchases.

G.I. Bill financing encouraged millions of American families to move out of urban areas to build new suburban homes.

We each had separate bedrooms but shared the kitchen, bathroom, and living room. There were shared household responsibilities like cleaning the house.

Although we all had different definitions of "clean."

Meal preparation rotated. We also had a different interpretation of what constituted a "meal."

We were three single guys earning more money than we've ever made with no place to spend it. The house hosted annual toga parties and weekly wild barbecues.

Our house became known as the 3003 Club, which was our address.

It was the reverse of *St. Elmo's Fire* (1985). Instead of Georgetown yuppie graduates, we were from the University of Wyoming, and our misadventures were redneck.

The people I ran around with in Gillette are among my best friends.

I adapted well to that wild and crazy co-op house experience. After having too much fun and some professional success, my next stop was 250 miles to the west in Lander.

Urban Urchin - Lander, Wyoming: "Where Rails End and Trails Begin" is the Lander tagline. The railroad did end. Lander was initially surveyed by General Frederick Lander and later founded as the southern gateway to Yellowstone National Park.

It's a sleepy town of 7,000 people at the foot of the majestic Wind River Mountains. The population hasn't changed much over the past 30 years.

I also worked for the city government. Due to a housing shortage, I found myself living downtown in the Faust apartments above the hardware store.

It wasn't really a shortage. The community was so stable that there were few housing choices for newcomers.

It was my first experience with mixed-use living.

At the time, I thought living downtown was the "low rent" district. The rent was more than reasonable for the apartment.

My space had a spacious living room with a bedroom and kitchen.

It was cozy.

Steam from one of those old-style cast iron radiators provided more than enough heat.

When it was hot, it was hot. The pipes banged, and the steam release valve hissed.

The one hallway was narrow. You couldn't help but bump into friendly neighbors. I befriended a guy who lived at the end of the hall.

He worked at the Wyoming Game and Fish Department. During the summer, he brewed bathtub beer.

We used to sit out on the back steps and sip a cold one as the irrigation stream gurgled in the small park below.

My bank was on one corner, the drug store on the opposite corner. The Grand movie theater was across the street, and my office was less than a block away. Behind my office was the grocery store.

I didn't drive locally for the year I lived downtown.

After that, I became an urban urchin and preferred the mixed-use downtown lifestyle before it became trendy.

...... ine Faust Apartments, I befriended another Alan and was a long-term house sitter for his small place near downtown.

He was a National Outdoor Leadership School (NOLS) instructor and was out in the bush for months at a time.

We got along pretty well as long as I kept the place up. I liked living alone, but together.

After moving to Colorado around 1993, the secret sauces I tasted in my past living arrangements readied me to eventually move into cohousing.

Sofa Surfer - Boulder, Colorado: My plan wasn't to move to Boulder. When I worked for the Northern Arapaho Tribe, my first Boulder visit was scouting a cultural exchange project.

The Northern Arapaho and Eastern Shoshone tribes share the Wind River Reservation in West-Central Wyoming. Lander is one of the border towns.

A local nonprofit organization collaborated with the Northern Arapaho tribe to create a "cultural conduit" that extended from the Reservation to Boulder.

The Estes Park to Boulder corridor was the traditional homeland of the Arapaho tribe.

The U.S. Army, led by Colonel John Chivington, massacred the Cheyenne and Arapaho tribes at Sand Creek on November 29, 1864. By treaty, both tribes were split up.

The Northern Arapaho were exiled north to Wyoming and the Northern Cheyenne to Montana. The other half of the tribal refugees were sent to Oklahoma.

The idea was to reestablish an Arapaho presence in Boulder. We worked with Boulder art gallery owners to free up exhibit space for Arapaho artists to show and sell their work.

Long story short, that project couldn't support itself mainly because many art galleries closed. The local nonprofit organization partner also went out of business.

Since I was a typical transient passing through Boulder, I spent months sofa-surfing with various friends I met.

Eventually, I decided to stay in Boulder. Like Lander, it was on the Front Range of the Rocky Mountains.

Plus, Boulder is 150 miles closer to Southeast Wyoming, where my family lived.

I was between sofas, and a spot opened up in a cooperative rental house with six people.

I knew the tenant who was moving out, and he referred me to Richard, the house organizer.

... the time, I was unaware of intentional communities other than the hippie commune that Dennis Hopper and Peter Fonda visit in the *Easy Rider* (1969) biker movie.

Having lived with housemates before in Gillette and Lander, living with other people wasn't that big of a deal.

The Hapgood House, as I called it, was a Buddhist-centered intentional community. We had house meetings when it came to vetting new housemates.

I wasn't a Buddhist practitioner, but our spiritual "higher purpose" made for an amicable and calm group without much conflict.

Based on this experience, if you're currently living in a cohousing community or thinking about it, one aspect of cohousing is glossed over.

At least discuss a "higher purpose" as a shared value for your community.

Community members need something that ties them together after the dander settles from stressful discussions about ferrets in the Common House or arguments about whether the carpet should be industrial-grade or shag.

The adventures of Robin Hood, who stole from the rich and gave to the poor, remind me of how a higher purpose transcends petty differences.

He and his merry men would come to blows and draw their swords.

When it came to a call to defeat the Sheriff of Nottingham, they dropped their weapons to take on a familiar foe.

The community's higher purpose doesn't have to be around spirituality or religion. There are plenty of secular reasons why a group of people would join together.

I think the higher purpose needs to be named so that events and deeds don't end up being "one-off" activities.

Maybe your higher purpose is advocating for lower-priced housing. Choose a summertime activity like volunteering on a local Habitat for Humanity project.

If your higher purpose is offering a hand-up to people who lost their jobs, how about the community members gathering up extra canned goods and donating them to the local food bank on a regular basis?

3a. Socialize and Help Out

If we want to build stronger relationships, we have to get up off the couch, participate in our cohousing neighborhoods, and help out the broader community.

There's a balance, though.

Neighbors weigh personal privacy and community participation by choosing their level of engagement, which is dynamic.

Collaborating with 30 strangers set in their ways is hard work. It's a trick juggling regular life and community life and figuring out the balance.

At SSV, most people are retired and have lots of spare time on their hands to devote to life in the community.

I'm still busy making movies and writing books. One of the newest residents is younger and works remotely.

SSV community business is a low priority for me. Retired people can attend meetings during what, for me, is the workday.

On the surface, being a part of the community, the social fabric seems straightforward, but personalities and other social dynamics can be detrimental to resident inclusion.

The quirks, mostly around control, have a place in Superman's American Way but are often problematic in collaborative decision-making.

If those personality traits are identified and redirected early during community formation, participation experiences can be more fulfilling.

I know of a cohousing community where a small group of residents worked their way into a project, took it over, and refused to give up power and control.

The community had to hire an impartial out-of-state facilitator to help the group through the problem. The same community also has two households that do not participate at all.

Getting the community work done is one of the ongoing topics of discussion at cohousing conferences.

Community jobs entail anything that a property management company would undertake on behalf of an HOA to incidental chores completed by residents.

Those tasks include ground maintenance like mowing the lawn, picking weeds, planting flowers, managing irrigation, and removing snow in winter.

If there's a clubhouse, jobs include cleaning the restrooms, checking the toilet paper, vacuuming rugs, and watering the plants.

There's also necessary financial management that includes keeping track of the HOA dues payments, paying the bills, and monitoring contractors.

Communities must also contend with emergencies like broken water pipes and gas leaks.

During routine and extraordinary times, managing a cohousing community requires an entire team effort.

I think the community formation stage is the best time for potential residents who may be disruptive to openly to self-identify themselves.

Disruption shows up in many ways.

Some disrupt by over-participating. Others are content to sit back and minimally participate or not participate at all. It would be good to know who they are, too.

Suppose you're going to invest your life savings into a cohousing neighborhood. I would want to know at least how my new neighbors may react in a stressful situation.

At SSV, my Coho Stout community, we live in private homes with all the usual amenities, including kitchens and living areas.

Coho Stout and Lite architects design homes that intentionally look out to the community and to have private spaces out of view.

Connecting with the community is easy and natural for residents but not required or constant.

Privacy matters, too. Shortly after I came back to SSV after being sick, I could not participate fully because of physical limitations.

Nor did I have the mental fitness to be engaged. I chose more privacy, and I dropped out of community duties.

I seldom made it to the potluck meals because nothing was appetizing. I didn't move around that great and couldn't fulfill Common House lock-up duty.

At the time, I was on the Community Enhancement Team and couldn't care less that Neighbor X was having an ongoing beef with Neighbor Y.

The privacy-community balance will look different if community members reside in an Ultra-Lite apartment building or a sub-community within a larger HOA.

I've talked about the importance of shared values. Relationships manifest themselves through community participation.

A year later, I started to get back into the swing of things and produced a documentary called *Aging Gratefully: The Power of Community* (2015).

That was the first in a series of, so far, six films about my illness and how the cohousing community stepped up to support me.

Subsequent episodes center around healthy social interactions, accidental communities, and the importance of culture in the community.

It was when I was sick that I understood the cohousing community social contract.

My partner in crime, Diana, was more familiar with cohousing. At the Farmer's Market, the SSV burning Souls sat at a booth, passing out information about an upcoming meeting. She dragged me along to get together for potential members. The development was several years out, and we immediately needed a place.

Instead, we chipped in on a townhouse in the Studio Mews housing area in the Holiday Neighborhood in North Boulder, Colorado.

She had two Welsh Corgi dogs that started having trouble hopping up and down the stairs.

Making that roundtrip several times a day was also a strain for my achy knees. It got to the point where I planned my daily up-and-down trips.

Diana moved her mother from Massachusetts to an assisted living community in Boulder.

Caring for her mom, she realized that a ground-level, one-story handicap-accessible home with no stairs or steps would be a better place to get old.

SSV cohousing was down the block, 600 feet away.

I think it was in the winter of 2008 that two SSV residents came trudging by while I was clearing snow off the sidewalk.

He wore one of those overly large and colorful Mad Hatter *chapeaus* and an open bottle of wine he poured into a paper cup.

"I'm Henry, and this is my wife, Jean," he said while handing me the wine and a calling card printed on an inkjet computer printer. "We just moved into Silver Sage Village from San Francisco."

Jean later developed Alzheimer's Disease. Henry claims she was able to stay at SSV for several years longer because of the community support she received before having to move into long-term memory care.

That was my first introduction to SSV.

Around that time, I was a member of the city of Boulder Planning Board and knew Jim Leach, the SSV developer.

He told me about a guy who died at SSV, and his heirs were having a hard time finding a new buyer.

I think that was because it was in the city of Boulder's housing program.

The pool of eligible people was limited, plus a buyer would have to want to live in a cohousing community.

The condo met Diana's housing checklist, and I blindly went along. We met the program criteria, were approved as tenants in common, and bought the place.

Cohousing communities build neighborliness by managing themselves and taking care of shared amenities like the courtyard and Common House.

The SSV community's recommended participation level is very manageable. Everyone is requested to be on one or two teams, lock up the Common House now, and attend the monthly full community meetings.

The SSV community HOA, because we are older and less able, contracts out much of the heavy lifting, like shoveling snow and mowing the lawn.

Even an outside contractor cleans the Common House.

In a sense, SSV contracts out weekly community meals since they are potluck. We seldom share in meal preparation, as is typical in many cohousing communities.

There are some hands-on duties like the Spring and Fall work days. My job is cleaning the barbecue grill.

During the summer, those who like to garden tend to flowers and plants. There are some maintenance tasks that the community tinkerers handle.

For the most part, as we've aged, our participation levels now include sitting in meetings writing rules, approving them, and then interpreting them.

Just about every task at SSV is a job and counts towards participation.

I mentioned that my next-door neighbor Jean developed Alzheimer's Disease. The community reserved emptying the dishwasher after community meals for her.

The newspapers are tossed onto porches and delivered in plastic sacks. SSV reuses those when replenishing the dog poop bags in the dispensers around the SSV perimeter.

The Common House team reserved that task for a resident with limited time to spare because of weird working hours.

Another community member liked to sort the small and large spoons and salad forks from the dinner forks into their appropriate baskets.

As the SSV community matured, members moved out or died, the average age climbed, and the people per square foot density declined.

If that trend continues, community participation will be more challenging with older and fewer residents.

For any community, look at yourselves as futurists and talk about this eventuality during your planning stages. What will your community be like in 20 or 30 years?

In a past life, I involved myself in a project that had to do with storing spent nuclear power reactor fuel rods called Monitored Retrievable Storage (MRS).

Various forms of Uranium have half-lives of 159,000 years. Radioactivity is long-lasting!

The U.S. Department of Energy held a workshop presented by a futurist about the importance of long-range planning.

MRS project managers needed to think about how to correctly mark the nuclear storage area for future generations when landmasses shift, and cultures and languages change.

Be a cohousing futurist. Will you have enough money in the reserve fund? When the founders are all dead and gone, are the tenets of cohousing institutionalized? Will cohousing take over the multi-family dwelling market sometime in the future?

Nobody thinks they are getting old until the community dinner small talk is about geriatrics and diseases rather than pediatrics and diseases.

Unlike a traditional HOA, cohousing HOAs are governed by all the owners instead of an elected board of directors.

Communities are self-governed by the residents using processes grounded in collaborative decision-making.

There are all sorts of consensus models. Pick an approach based on your community's needs. There is no "best solution." SSV is relatively small and views itself as a community of teams and not individuals.

Any issue brought to the community is referred to a team that works out the details before our Steering Team, akin to the Board of Directors, determines if the issue is vetted adequately for a community decision for consideration and approval by consensus.

SSV functions very well with a basic consensus process. Larger communities may opt for a more structured model.

Consensus decision-making is slow, clunky, and requires patience. There are consensus skeptics who think that a conspiracy of the few can stop decisions. SSV allows for "blockers" who can stall a decision only if they state their position, so it is about why their "block" is in the best interest of the entire community, not just self-interest.

In going on 20 years, SSV has never had a decision blocked. I recall two residents who, upon their blocks being overridden, said they would not participate in implementing the particular policy. In the vernacular of the cohousing locker room, they took their ball and went home.

Compared to winning-by-one espoused by Superman's American Way, figuring out how to use the consensus process is a learned behavior.

Becoming uncompetitive is not natural.

An entire industry cropped up around assisting communities to learn consensus.

I've done a few workshops around facilitating a group through the consensus process that entails mish-mashing together information that requires not just "majority rules" but "unanimous rules."

If you're a cat owner, you'll understand the reference that building consensus is like "herding cats."

If your agreed-upon decision-making method doesn't work, change it and try again.

Decision-making fits into any consensus template, but outlying issues that are contentious or unknown are the ones that cause the most angst, mainly if they come up at the last minute.

All cohousing community HOAs meet at least monthly, but sometimes urgent decisions have to be made during the interim.

There are real emergencies and elective emergencies.

A real emergency affecting the community would include a gas leak or a broken water line, which is straightforward.

As a general rule, I'd say that most communities have mechanisms to deal with community health and safety-related emergencies, including unannounced entry into a residence.

Elective emergencies are different. Those can be around some sort of self-interested convenience and could have been resolved earlier.

Elective emergencies become immediate when the request is brought forward at the last minute and a solution is demanded "right now."

In some cases, elective emergencies do require immediate action.

Early in your community formation, establish a shared value that it's okay for residents to bring forth matters that may appear on the surface to be self-interested.

"I think 'all lives matter,' not just Black lives," a guy in a Wyoming-based Zoom meeting said. Wyoming is my home state and is very conservative.

My response was about a time when I was growing up in Cheyenne.

My Cole Addition neighborhood was idyllic and typical 1960s suburbia.

It was oddly diverse, with several Japanese and Greek families within a block or two of each other. We had strong extended families.

All the neighbors knew each other because all the kids attended the same school. In the summer, backyard barbecue dinners that rotated from house to house.

The community was very cohesive.

One day, my next-door neighbor, Alex, rang the bell and asked if my parents were home.

They were not. Later, I learned that Alex's brother had died. He had three generations living together in his home, including a grandmother called Yaya.

My mom brought over a covered dish, as did all the other neighbors. We all mourned for Alex and his family.

Most of the time, all neighbors mattered, but for a while, Alex's family mattered more.

When an elective emergency is brought forth by a community member, it may seem self-interested.

A community request may need attention because one neighbor's circumstance matters more at that moment, even if approving the proposal is contrary to a shared value or impinges on the other community members' rights.

SSV had a community retreat led by a facilitator named Yana Ludwig, who lived in an intentional community in Laramie, Wyoming, at the time.

She shed some light on ways to avoid last-minute elective emergencies by being proactive.

Identifying outlier counter-perspectives can derail projects or ideas that many community members may have previously agreed to by expressing their opinions.

Yana referred to "Bubbles" as all points of view that should be considered before making final decisions.

After all the diverse bubbles are identified, scribe a "Box" or "Boxes" around as many bubbles as practical to determine the best solution that considers the outlier views.

Each box you draw is a possible solution.

In a consensus community, all points are not just heard but taken into consideration.

The few who may oppose or favor an idea or proposal to the point of blocking it (Bubble Blockers), in my view, are the ones who need to have the most attention paid to them.

Community members shouldn't view Bubble Blockers as bad neighbors who gum up the works.

A Bubble Blocker may be a new and better perspective. Adding that Bubble Blocker to the mix may result in a better decision.

Bubble Blockers should position their perspectives in terms of how it affects the entire community for maximum effectiveness.

In my experience, because consensus decision-making is so diffuse, self-interested bubbles are the ones that cause the most angst in the consensus-making process.

That's the "cat herding" part.

I'd estimate that 99 percent of all the decisions a community makes are routine and have little or no controversy because those decisions benefit all.

An example of a one-bubble, one-box decision at SSV would be the proposal to spend several thousand dollars installing the photovoltaic solar panels on the roof that generate more than enough Common House electricity.

The community agreed to that proposal with little discussion and dissent because the improvement benefited everyone.

Most issues that arise in a cohousing community are petty to the casual outside observer but might as well be the brink of nuclear war inside the community.

Not that I'm any kind of psychologist, but my observation is that people generally avoid conflict whenever they can, including putting off tough decisions.

Early in my local government career, I attribute my success to isolating and solving potential problems before they escalate and shut down ideas or projects.

When I worked for a domestic violence prevention organization, I learned that my problem-solving approach is "crisis intervention." In the context of consensus decision-making, I see it as engaging Bubble Blockers.

The community may identify Bubble Blockers ahead of time, resulting in medium or soft-hard feelings rather than super-hard feelings.

Because cohousing decision-making is so diffuse, the most contentious issues tend to be self-interested requests.

Landscaping is a common source of conflict in cohousing communities. I'll use the example of mature tree removal to open up one household's view.

The process can result in several months of angst and high conflict.

A Bubble Blocker may say removing a tree is too expensive and the change only benefits one household.

How might that be resolved?

Maybe a Bubble Blocker moves toward consensus by saying that removing the tree is okay if the applicant compensates the community for the loss.

That could include the costs of removal and replacement. If it's a big tree, there are appraisal services that determine the value of old trees.

In the real world, government agencies require mining companies to post a reclamation bond and chip into a severance tax fund that "pays for" taking the irreplaceable mineral for corporate gain.

If a consensus can be reached about a view's monetary worth, financial compensation to the community could avoid a major conflict.

Another typical HOA political issue concerns pets. At a regular HOA, the homeowners elect a board of directors to act on their behalf.

That HOA board may pass a policy that says "no pets" or "no cigarette smoking." The board holds sole authority, and that's the end of the discussion.

In the case of a cohousing pet policy, decision-making is decentralized and allows more opportunities for members to request exceptions.

Over the years, the SSV community made exceptions to the "no pets in the Common House" rule.

One ongoing exception allows that if the weather is terrible or a pet is infirm, upstairs dogs can use the elevator to come through the Common House.

Another case was a short-term exception. A community-wide repair meant all owners had to move out of their homes for an extended period of time.

When residents vacated their condos, two residents were allowed to keep a dog and a cat in the Common House for a few weeks during the construction.

A third exception was after an arduous community discussion that resulted in two cats being allowed to live in the guest room, which was vacated during the pandemic.

Before the community gets too far in the decision-making process, at least discuss potential self-interested and contentious issues before they arise.

Crisis interventions can do wonders by tempering arguments before they escalate.

Let's say a neighbor is having some interior design work done that will take a few months, and they want to keep their pet ferret in the Common House.

Identify the Bubble Blockers ahead of time. In the case of the pet ferret, Blockers may have concerns about the animal's health and welfare.

Another Blocker says they are allergic to ferrets. A third Blocker wonders what happens if the critter gets loose and the ferret wranglers can't coax it out of the kitchen pantry.

Each community has its share of Bubble Blockers and their issues. Taking time to work through concerns brings creative solutions that work for all, not just the majority.

Managing and maintaining the shared property empowers residents, builds community, and can save money through efficiency.

The COVID-19 self-isolation measures changed how cohousing community members participated in socially interactive meetings and workdays in the garden.

Much of the SSV official business conducted in live meetings had moved into online Zoom rooms. Most other cohousing communities did the same.

The PDX Commons community in Portland, Oregon, was designed with the condos constructed to face a courtyard. During COVID-19, residents continued to interact with their neighbors across the open common space while physically isolated.

I was one of the more risk-averse members and didn't participate in live activities. Those included outdoor community dinners. We went through the "bring your own meals" phase. That evolved into the potluck but with the dishes served rather than self-served.

During the winter, the heartiest community members dined in the courtyard and kept warm by sitting among natural gas heaters, like those used at outdoor restaurants.

Participants observed social distancing on garden days in the spring and summer. Weeders and trimmers wore masks.

After social distancing was no longer in force, reentry to face-to-face activities was novel at first. I felt naked without a mask. I still carry one folded up in my wallet.

I've learned over the years that there's nothing like a good old-fashioned crisis to bring a community of any size together.

You may meet your neighbor for the first time due to a power outage during a massive snowstorm or become closer to your cohousing residents during the COVID-19 pandemic.

Cohousing communities and residents are well equipped to deal with crises, such as implementing COVID-19 prevention measures.

Working together is the definition of cohousing.

In February, one of my neighbors, Lindy, a Registered Nurse, monitored COVID-19 before it became mainstream.

She convened two community meetings to discuss the virus and its potential impact on SSV.

CohoUS and most cohousing communities were also resilient and ahead of the pandemic curve.

In June 2019, CohoUS changed its business cycle by organizing a series of smaller, web-based conferences as a revenue generator in the national conference off years.

As a result of this now prophetic change, by the spring of 2020, CohoUS had figured out Zoom technology well before other businesses could respond to the COVID-19 pandemic.

Shortly after Lindy's SSV presentation, CohoUS convened a national Zoom conference call attended by over 100 people who shared their community's best practices.

If you go into the Common House today, I think the flip chart she wrote up still exists as a pandemic artifact. Her analysis was right on the money.

SSV was a microcosm of what was happening in the outside world.

At the March 2020 community meeting, The SSV residents arrived at a consensus about how to implement social distancing and stay-at-home orders by balancing individual self-interests with those of the community as a whole.

"I'm not worried" to "This is a hoax" to "Put on the Haz-Mat suits" was the range of SSV member perspectives.

Those diverse opinions also were evident in day-to-day behavior. Some of the more cavalier neighbors sometimes wore or didn't wear masks. Some members relied on Dr. Google to research articles and stories to plant doubt in our minds, similar to the tobacco companies' efforts to tell us that smoking wasn't as bad as the real scientists would lead us to believe.

Others were vigilant and masked up all the time.

National perspectives politicizing mask-wearing caused angst around the community about personal liberty vs. the common good.

Those conversations abruptly ended when two of my neighbors came down with COVID-19 upon their return from what was a super-spreader family event.

Despite philosophical differences, community dinners took place during the chillier and darker months.

SSV purchased five propane heaters, the same type that keeps outdoor seating areas warm at ski areas.

Myself? I'm more of a "Business as usual" guy and was far from being "freaked out." I dutifully attend the online community meetings in Zoom rooms.

I didn't take part in any face-to-face meetups since I considered myself a member of the vulnerable population as a pneumonia survivor. Plus, I'm old and a guy.

During the early days of the pandemic, I offered to fulfill Common House duties for those unwilling to leave their homes. I helped out two neighbors. One was sick after returning from a trip to the East Coast and was self-isolated.

The other neighbor I helped out was Lindy, the nurse, who was also one of the most vigilant neighbors and homebound.

My goodwill stopped when a not-so-active community member tried taking advantage of my good nature by asking me to pick up her slack for some bogus reason.

SSV duty is light and includes checking the Common House exterior doors and watering the plants.

Internationally, nationally, and locally, hyper-vigilance and defiance created political heroes and villains, increased ratings on cable TV talking heads shows, and sold more toilet paper. Still, in the long run, lives were saved, and social and cultural divides were moved to the forefront.

We cohousers are predisposed to be hedges against isolation through collaboration, sharing of time and resources, and keeping track of one another.

The pandemic hit home with me when one of my cousins in Illinois died from exposure to an asymptomatic COVID-19 carrier. He buried his mom - my aunt - in July and was hospitalized shortly after that and died on August 3, 2022.

Diana's granddaughter was a 4th-grade school teacher and contracted the virus. She was in quarantine at home.

SSV was generally compliant with the Boulder County mandates. Some neighbors self-isolated because of illness, returned home from travel, or were just cautious.

Self-isolation didn't deter the community from getting together, particularly around COVID-19.

Every month during isolation, the SSV community convened in a Zoom room and reviewed the COVID-19 guidelines. We updated them by consensus as necessary.

My routine didn't change much. I write books and make movies, which entails quite a bit of time in front of a computer screen.

Plus, during the business day, I'm in meetings and writing groups with people from around the country and the globe.

I live a mushroom existence in my office, COVID or no COVID.

In the evenings, I caught up on pandemic-related movies and TV shows.

I watched *Outbreak* (1995) on Prime video with Dustin Hoffman and Rene Russo playing two scientists. Stopping the deadly virus brings the estranged couple back together.

On Netflix, I watched a TV series called *Containment* (2015) about what happens among frustrated people during a viral outbreak in an Atlanta quarantine area where there are too many "rats in a cage."

Next was the classic *Andromeda Strain* (1971). A virus from outer space is defeated after observant scientists determine that a person's fluid acidity is the most effective treatment.

Then there was *Contagion* (2015) with Gwyneth Paltrow. The movie goes backward in time and is about contact tracing.

At SSV, my COVID-19 behavior was observing the lowest common denominator, which was hyper-vigilance and wearing a mask indoors and outdoors.

SSV community COVID-19 guidelines generally prohibited outsiders from entering the Common House. Community members minimized their Common House trips. That wasn't much different from pre-pandemic.

The guest room was closed during the pandemic and converted into the cattery before it became an office space.

Before the pandemic, to monetize the underutilized Common House, SSV has had long-term users in an artist coworking space and rented office spaces, including one for my business, Boulder Community Media.

Before COVID-19, the building was primarily used by outside groups who rented the Common House space for meetings and parties.

Like other businesses during the pandemic, SSV limited the outside groups that would have normally rented the Common House.

Revenues dropped considerably as a result of COVID-19. Since then, we've had to be creative about ways to stabilize revenues.

The community is evaluating how other under-utilized spaces can be monetized, such as additional offices, an apartment for another resident, or quarters for a property/personal caretaker.

Since its founding, SSV members haven't frequented the Common House much, other than picking up their mail, convening team meetings the third week of each month, and sharing dinner twice a week.

Because most of the condos at SSV are so large, there is less of a need for those residents to use the Common House to entertain or socialize.

My observation is that those who live in the smaller SSV units frequent the Common House kitchen, dining area, craft room, and TV room much more because their living areas are limited.

All things being equal, size matters. For forming traditional Coho Stout communities, take a page out of Sarah Susanka's book.

Communities with more condos that are smaller and closer in size to one another ultimately result in more equitable HOA dues and higher use of the Common House.

Participation also means random encounters with neighbors that continued on a smaller scale during the pandemic.

The SSV community social distancing policy wasn't much of an inconvenience, but the number of spontaneous barbecues and happy hours significantly declined.

Regardless of their perspectives about the gravity of the pandemic, all community members had to alter their behaviors.

Most Baby Boomers, including myself, were around during the 1950s and 1960s toward the end of the polio pandemic.

My family supported the public health policies when the oral polio vaccines came out.

One kid recovered from polio in my grade school and wore a leg brace like the young *Forrest Gump* (1994).

His hip-swiveling was an inspired Elvis, who stayed in their extra bedroom in the Oscar-winning movie.

School bullies pushed around my classmate because he also wore a hearing aid. Back then, they were very conspicuous, with earphones wired to a receiver the size of a Band-Aid box.

Jonas Salk developed the first vaccine, which was administered by injection. Getting jabbed with what seemed to be a needle the size of a railroad spike was my first shot. I don't remember being freaked out about it.

Back in the 1960s, the vaccine development competition was fierce. In the case of polio, Albert Sabin won the oral vaccine contest.

Polio vaccines were risky because some people vaccinated contracted polio, but the number of cases prevented outweighed the risk of death and illness.

I remember a big family social event was gathering at my grandparents' house on East 8th Street in the Southside of Cheyenne.

We walked over to the fire station and stood in line with all the other neighbors to get a sugar cube with the pink vaccine fluid dropped onto it.

It seems like there were boosters necessary, but the most memorable was the first one.

During the polio pandemic, there was a high level of societal consensus about eradicating polio. There was no blame placed on any social or racial groups for the disease's origin. Instead, polio was a Commie plot that had to be stopped. Any self-respecting American could get behind that.

What about the swine flu (H1N1-09) that swept the globe in 2009? Any lessons learned from H1N1-09 were in my rearview mirror. I had to look up to refresh my memory.

The spread of that virus coincided with a financial system collapse and the home financing crisis.

That was a pretty big deal but wasn't politicized like COVID-19. I read that the first H1N1-09 cases in the

United States originated in Mexico. President 45 would have been all over that.

H1N1-09 was viewed as a public health threat and not a way to score political points. On top of it all, President Barack Obama had a lot on his plate back then, keeping the auto industry afloat and the banks stable.

Obama eventually declared H1N1-09 a national emergency. It was a similar virus to the 1918 flu virus.

Doctors initially treated H1N1-09 with the regular flu vaccine, which was 56 percent effective. Grocery store products like Tylenol and Advil were helpful in treating symptoms.

Nonetheless, 500,000 people died, and a billion were sick around the world.

There were warnings about the H1N1-09 contagion, but no mass closures of schools or businesses, nor were employees self-isolating in mass numbers.

Cohousers had the wherewithal to fast-track hyper-vigilant responses to control public health and safety crises because of the high level of cooperation.

In the early days of the pandemic, certain foods and household products were hoarded. Boulderites are stereotyped as being very health-conscious and making wise food choices.

You wouldn't have thought that based on the store inventory. The SPAM and Beefaroni shelves were empty.

I don't know about you, but I still have plenty of toilet paper stashed under the bed and in the bathroom cabinet to last me until the next pandemic.

I'm an organized hoarder, and that's a throwback to my childhood. My family had quite a routine for stocking up the fallout shelter during the Cold War.

I ate up all my emergency food when I bought it. Next crisis, I'll stock up on my least favorite snacks.

I mentioned meeting my neighbor during a snowstorm.

When I moved to Laramie for graduate school in 1976 and lived at my parents' townhouse, there was a power outage.

My neighbor was out on the walk. He was a fellow University of Wyoming alumnus and a former linebacker for the football team.

We both checked out the aftermath of the winter blizzard. Snow had drifted to the side of our houses. Neither of us had power.

He introduced himself. It was none other than Conrad Dobler, pro football's "Dirtiest Player."

He and his family lived in Laramie during the offseason when he wasn't on the field, playing for the St. Louis football Cardinals.

Conrad turned out to be a pretty nice guy, and if you do anything over the next few weeks, get to know your neighbors, even if it's from six feet away.

Your lives may one day depend on new-found friends and established relationships.

Cohousing and bomb shelters: In the cohousing community, we've agreed upon how to support one another in the event of illness, lack of food, and when cleaning supplies are short.

The SSV Common House and that of the Wild Sage Cohousing community across the street are pretty good large-scale places for others in the neighborhood to shelter in place if need be. More likely in the event of a bad storm.

As a course of our day-to-day cohousing lives, the community keeps stores of paper towels, toilet paper, and cleaning supplies on hand.

I want to refine our civil protection protocol now that the COVID-19 thing has blown over.

The SSV community mutual pandemic support that's come about today is a lot like how things were back during the Cold War.

My family and extended family were tight-knit enough to hunker down together while preparing for the impending nuclear war.

We were the only household in the neighborhood to build a "fallout" shelter. In 1964, Barry Goldwater didn't rule out the use of atomic bombs to end the Vietnam War.

My dad was the military hawk in the family. I'm pretty sure he voted for Goldwater, which may be one reason for our family civil defense project.

The early stages of the COVID-19 pandemic posed a public health and safety threat similar to Civil Defense preparedness during the Cold War.

After initial international and national tension, friends and foes soon worked together to slow the viral spread.

COVID-19 should have been pretty easy to build consensus around stomping out a terrible virus. The battle against polio was viewed as a protecting American democracy. The COVID-19 virus became politicized, causing major divisions among the citizenry at home and abroad.

Baby Boomers and older likely remember October 1963 when the USSR installed nuclear missiles in Cuba in response to the botched Bay of Pigs invasion to take back Cuba from Fidel Castro.

There was a political standoff between President John Kennedy and USSR premier Nikita Khrushchev.

After Khrushchev backed down to JFK and the nuclear weapons were removed from Cuba, tensions decreased, even though the United States and Russia continued to escalate the arms race.

The Cuban missile crisis lessened the nuclear war threat. Americans were more aware and vigilant due to preparations for an unforeseen war.

While I was growing up, Cheyenne had the highest concentration of nuclear missiles in the country.

Francis E. Warren Air Force Base was the command center for the Atlas missile program following World War II.

The Department of Defense figured out that a better way to deploy nuclear weapons was to install lighter-weight nuclear warheads on rockets.

Missile installation was a booming industry in middle-of-nowhere places like Southeast Wyoming.

Not that we would be any safer, my parents decided to build a bomb shelter in the basement of our home in the Cole Addition, one of the suburbs on Cheyenne's east side.

I imagine the bomb shelter was for peace of mind more than anything since a missile hitting a cornfield in the

Nebraska panhandle would be considered a direct hit on Cheyenne.

Bill Fisher was one of the guys who worked for my dad at the Coke plant. My dad paid him a few bucks to help us build the bomb shelter.

He was a veteran of World War II and the Korean War and lived in the basement of a partially constructed house. Part of the foundation was poured but not completed. I think he was a squatter.

There were dirt caves where he kept stuff. I was never quite sure what to make of Bill living underground in a series of tunnels.

He was a hermit. Maybe that was Post Traumatic Stress Disorder (PTSD)-related, but Bill knew a lot about science.

He worked around the plant, sorting the Coke from the Sprite bottles and helping on the production line.

His main job was working on the Coke product vending machine refrigeration systems.

Bill's place was across the street from the Coke plant. When I went to work with my dad on Saturdays, I goofed around inside the plant but eventually made my way over to visit Bill.

He subscribed to "Things of Science," an educational program launched by the nonprofit news syndicate Science Service in November 1940.

The program consisted of a series of kits that were available by subscription and sent by mail monthly.

The Science Service packed each kit in a small blue cardboard box with yellow lettering about the size of a portable external hard drive with an address label.

Included inside was a simple science project. I remember one being a crystal radio set, and another was a small motor run on electromagnetic current, battery not included.

Bill had the little boxes categorized by year and stacked up on a ledge in a niche carved into the dirt wall of his literal "man cave."

One Christmas, he bought me a subscription. The cost was $5.00 for the year.

He was a quiet guy. Since he had no family, Bill was always invited over to our place for Thanksgiving.

On our way to the grandparents' homes for Christmases 2 and 3, we always stopped by to see Bill and drop off a gift and some food.

Anyway, Bill had researched bomb shelters and helped build ours. Bill was also a very meticulous mason.

He taught me how to mix mortar and lay blocks, which are life skills I've used on occasion over the years.

According to Bill's information, he located the shelter in the northeast corner of the basement at the bottom of the stairs, making for easy access.

There was also a window well that led to the outside. Bill made an air shaft by welding steel pipes inside the shelter and vented to the exterior.

A set of surplus bunk beds was set up against one wall across from a pantry, where I rotated the stored canned goods with new items from the kitchen. We kept the tableware in a cabinet.

The fallout shelter temperature was always the same, and it was an excellent place to hang out during hot summer days.

We had a small Sterno camping stove that wasn't very practical in an enclosed space, but there was a place to set it up by the air vent.

We had a downstairs bathroom. Before the bomb shelter project, Bill did the plumbing.

He taught me how to make a "sweat joint" while connecting the water line to the sink. That's another life skill that was useful later in life.

So that we wouldn't have to risk exposure to harmful fallout walking down the hall to the bathroom, the shelter toilet was a galvanized steel port-a-potty with a sealed cover.

The threat of nuclear attack was real but mostly theoretical.

The main reason for the shelter was protection from "fallout," the residual radioactive dust spewed into the upper atmosphere following a nuclear blast and eventually would fall back to earth.

The amount and spread of fallout are based on the weapon's size, the altitude at which it is detonated, and prevailing winds.

Since Cheyenne is so windy, locals thought the breeze would blow any fallout to Nebraska and Colorado.

"Do not look at the fireball," the short Civil Defense movies warned us about how to prepare for a nuclear attack.

There were air raid drills similar to fire drills, except we sheltered in place. One exercise was diving under the desks and covering our heads with our hands or a jacket.

We also practiced exiting the classroom and going down into the school boiler room shelter staffed by the custodian, Mr. Costello.

I liked going to the grocery store with my mom during the summertime.

Not that I like shopping, I stood in the cereal aisle looking at the backs of all the Post cereal boxes with panels of baseball cards.

I spent many hours perusing for the ones that had the most New York Yankees players, particularly Mickey Mantle and Roger Maris.

Sometimes, that meant tossing cereal boxes in the cart that I didn't like.

After returning home from the store, one of my jobs was to rotate the bomb shelter canned goods out and replace them with the new stock.

The cans were dated using a Magic Marker. I'm still a food hoarder based on those days. Rather than buying one can of Beefaroni, I get four.

My dad and I spent Saturdays making the rounds at the two local war surplus, Goodwill and Salvation Army stores, looking for items that would make a living in the bomb shelter with creature comforts like extra can openers and cooking utensils.

Since my preparation for nuclear, I'm very aware of disaster contingency planning.

A big flood swamped Boulder in September 2013.

SSV remained dry, except that the detention pond was filled to the brim from neighborhood runoff. When the sun came out, I took a walk around the neighborhood. Flood water devastated property a few blocks west and south.

According to the Federal Emergency Management Agency (FEMA) maps, SSV is slightly above the flood plain.

Not only was it an unusually wet summer, but the western United States was on fire, including 10 miles from Boulder.

The Cal-Wood Fire crept to within five miles of SSV. The flames jumped U.S. Highway 36. In case authorities evacuated North Boulder, I had an emergency bag packed that included some of my best baseball cards.

We were out of harm's way, but streams of cars were heading to Boulder from the evacuation zones.

A few years ago, SSV purchased an array of photovoltaic solar panels that provide electricity for the Common House. We could add batteries to store the excess power generated.

Even though every one of my SSV neighbors had a similar experience with Civil Defense and nuclear preparedness during the 1960s, I haven't been able to convince them that using the SSV Common House basement would be a safe haven for flood and fire evacuees.

I'll have to make it someone else's idea.

I want to begin emergency event planning for the SSV community. I don't think we need to worry about nuclear war, but the changing weather patterns may require shelter from high winds, floods, and who knows what else, maybe locusts.

Since SSV residents seldom use the Common House kitchen, the pantry is a storage closet. The refrigerator shelves are also bare.

I'll check to see if the community is open to stocking a few food staples that would benefit everyone and others who may need shelter during times of emergency.

The other day, Diana and I sorted out our pantry to set up a place to store food in our storage space in the Common House basement.

The community has been reviewing a safety audit. I've been getting community input about our safety plan and want to update it with emergency preparedness.

Fast forward seven years when COVID-19 wandered onto the scene. Virus information wasn't consistent, and urban legends were rampant. The conspiracy theorists blamed China. The national debate led by a former President revolved around finger-pointing, more so than how to protect ourselves against contracting it.

Early on, SSV was equally confused. Some of my neighbors didn't think COVID-19 was any big deal. The disease might have been taken more seriously if it resulted in black sores or skin sloughing off, like in the movies.

The naysayers attended the community dinners unmasked with hubris, while others had self-isolated since the beginning.

Over time, the community **approved guidelines** concerning the use of the Common House.

Most of my neighbors came around to being more vigilant, didn't go out much, and observed social distancing when talking to neighbors.

When Colorado Governor Jared Polis ordered Coloradans to stay home, our cohousing community observed the suggested safety measures.

Like everywhere else, there were runs on food and toilet paper. Most of the grocery stores offered early-morning "senior hours" so we old folks could avoid being caught in stampedes. Since we're all well over 60 here and in the "vulnerable" demographic, we were given more flexibility.

SSV planned a big outdoor party in the courtyard to celebrate one neighbor's 80th birthday in the summer of 2021 and hoped the prevailing winds would keep any airborne COVID-19 away.

Even if they didn't, I had peace of mind knowing that there was a stash of toilet paper in the Common House basement. The party was canceled.

Chronic over and underachievement: If there's anything that bogs down a collaborative community, it's the few people who put their noses everywhere and, on the opposite end, those who are seldom seen.

The extremes are problematic in cohousing communities and any group that relies on shared participation to move its mission forward.

When it comes to participation, SSV residents are asked to occasionally check the Common House doors at night and sign up for one or two teams that match their interests.

If you're a numbers wonk, maybe the finance team would be good for you. Handy people who like to fix leaky faucets may find a place on the maintenance team.

I was a little kid soccer coach in a past life. In that game, the most skilled players pass the ball and are less selfish team leaders, which opens up more opportunities to win games.

A player who hogs the ball may be skilled but maximizes their individual role, ignoring the other 10 players on the field. That type of play is very limiting and, thus, decreases scoring chances.

Players who stand around or shy away from the game action also detract from the team, causing others to cover their area on the field.

Like my youth soccer team, community members should share the workload. If everyone does their part, jobs are completed more efficiently and in a timely manner.

More people sharing their perspectives results in creative solutions rather than those based on a single point of view.

In my high school, there were "chronic overachievers." I was one of those annoying kids on every page of the yearbook, newspaper staff 1,2,3, student senate 1,2,3, art club 1,2,3, … etc.

My parents had the "talk" with me as a Baby Boomer Japanese American adolescent about how to avoid the overt and unsaid discrimination I would face in the world.

That socialization process is partially to blame for my overachieving tendencies. Those pointers included everything I did that was bad would be noticed. Anything I did well would go unnoticed.

I wanted to keep my parents happy and didn't want to screw up.

As a result, I became a tactical chronic overachiever because I became tired of being passed over. I had to do more and try harder to keep up with kids I viewed as less skilled than me.

I honed my skills by joining activities where I could excel as an individual and didn't involve being "picked" to be a member of a team.

Those singular activities included carving out a spot on the newspaper staff as the cartoonist beginning in junior high school and a skill that lasted through college.

In sports, I became a pretty good 107-pound wrestler. In softball, I gave up the infield in favor of learning how to be the catcher. Nobody liked to catch.

Some people, as adults, haven't shaken their over or underachievement personality traits. In cohousing, it's no different.

I view community participation as an important duty that each of us fulfills when we enter into the cohousing social contract. I say "duty" because participation should occur "no matter what" as part of the social contract each member has with one another.

There are other things I'd rather do than sit in team and community meetings for two hours.

Early in your community formation, when nobody knows one another very well, is an excellent time to figure out who wants to help out on every task and those who are happy to sit back.

If that tendency is allowed to continue unchecked, just like in high school, there are fewer tasks for others to do or more jobs others have to complete to make up for those who don't participate.

"Sally is good at that. She can do it." Like the ball hog on my soccer teams, complacency can take over. If one of the overachievers suddenly quits, moves, or worse, those actions create voids.

I advocated cross-training team leaders by establishing a rotation. That resulted in pushback from one of the control freaks, who jumped ship and resurfaced as the team lead for a new team they helped establish.

That community member later realized they had gotten over their head. Cross-training rotating leads is now the community norm.

I'm a passive participator at SSV and put in the minimum effort so nobody has to do my jobs. I satisfy my over-achieving tendencies outside the community, where I volunteer for several nonprofit organizations and public boards and commissions.

Residents who don't participate or hold up their fair share of the duty can create jealousy and bitterness.

Cohousing communities govern themselves through a flat organizational structure, as opposed to a top-down transactional approach.

Placing too much authority in the hands of a few may work for the railroads. In senior cohousing, each of us is one deep vein blood clot away from being a vegetable.

Early on, your forming community should discuss and agree that sharing responsibilities is not about taking away personal power.

Collaboration adds better controls around a leadership style that brings out the best in each teammate.

Sharing the work is more important in a senior cohousing community as mental and physical abilities wane.

All should agree about sharing the workload and discouraging a handful of people who volunteer to do most of the work. There's no extra credit for doing more work.

On the other hand, there may be reasons why passive participators may be holding back. If it gets to be too many, that can be problematic.

Whether a resident is an over or underachiever, residents should remember their caring and sharing roles when it comes to getting to the root of the problem.

This is where the personality test can be useful. Maybe there are personal reasons: dislike of other members, preferring to work alone rather than as a team, employment responsibilities, or mental illness.

I think participation should be consistent and fair, but flexible. If an SSV resident can't participate at the minimum level, they can appeal to the Steering team. In my view, proving you have a deficit is demeaning.

I've had to apply for food stamps and unemployment benefits. Proving you're poor is degrading.

The humiliation factor may be why nobody has bothered to appeal for a change to their community participation responsibilities.

Maybe it's not a big deal if people do more or less as long as the work gets done.

3b. Accept and Reach Out

Superman's American Way and societal pressures about individuality and striving for material success can stifle community values.

Cohousers reinvent Superman's American Way by theoretically becoming more aware of socio-economic differences. We may not take the steps necessary to bridge cultural differences, but at least they are on our minds.

Lack of awareness can stifle care for neighbors and acceptance of those different, hindering efforts to build an inclusive community embedded into the broader culture.

Superman's American Way is pounded into our heads from the moment we glance up from the hospital bassinet and stare at the obstetrician for the first time.

Reaching out to others isn't a part of our cultural DNA.

When I get snippy in an email thread, there are short-term negative repercussions. The community holds me accountable by pointing out our shared value, to be nice.

The question is, could cohousing exist without email?

When a cohousing community mixes up a batch of secret sauce, I think the "shared values" ingredient is the most difficult to get in the proper proportions.

Being a cohouser means learning to taste the world with a cleansed palate.

What do I mean by that? Living with shared values in a consensus community is antithetical to Superman's overachieving American Way.

I recall mentioning in a community discussion that we all have to check our egos at the door when entering the cohousing world.

"I like to take on many tasks because I enjoy serving the community," was one overachiever perspective. They didn't think their choices to do more than expected took opportunities away from others.

Two groups, the Conflict Resolution Group and the Design Review Team, require members to be elected by secret ballot. In my view, that contradicts the SSV transparency value.

I'll characterize the voting as popularity contests. If you're one of the "cool kids" you're more be picked. Those processes take away more participation opportunities and serve to build the overachievers' list of titles.

"I have to take all the meeting minutes because nobody else has the skills to do it," another said about their desire to control information. Be sure to read the minutes to be sure that meeting proceedings are recorded accurately.

The challenge is figuring out how to blend the secret sauce with sweet and sour ingredients, which entails giving up individual rights and sharing rather than taking.

- Inclusion of marginalized people or no diversity
- Gentle on the earth or an overconsuming lifestyle
- Value personal differences or monocultural
- Senior community members or multigenerational residents

Close cultural divides: I suggest you seriously discuss among yourselves about why you personally - as opposed to philosophically - want lower-cost housing or diversity in your community.

As you form your community or if you're updating your existing community shared values, get firm commitments about everyone being willing to possibly fork out additional cash to level the field for those who cannot otherwise afford to live there.

On a personal level, ask yourself whether you're willing to put in the work to examine your perspectives and change them if necessary.

Be aware that lower-priced housing also means demographic and social diversity.

"We have diversity in our community. Three of our members drive blue, red, and green Subarus," is a joke around cohousing circles. "We have diversity here. All of us graduated from different Ivy League colleges."

Data generated by the CRN found that among a sample of a rental cohousing community, residents were more likely to consist of single parents, earn low to moderate incomes, and be persons of color.

COVID-19 exacerbated an already short supply of cost-efficient housing. As a public good, figuring out how to provide shelter to others may be on your radar screens as your community forms.

The other day, I watched *Jurassic Park* (1995), which is about genetically modified dinosaurs going berserk in a reality theme park.

One of the movie themes espoused by a scientist (Jeff Goldblum) is ecosystem unpredictability–chaos theory.

Random behavior may explain the rapid rise in COVID-19 infections. The COVID-19 ecosystem became intertwined with the human environment.

There was plenty of anecdotal information out in cyberspace about how COVID-19 isolation caused more people to be depressed, become more domestically violent, and otherwise expose personal needs to release internalized feelings.

Whether or not COVID-19 chaos caused a Minneapolis police officer to suffocate an African American named George Floyd to death is anyone's guess. The incident sparked racial unrest and some riots across the country.

Concerned pent-up citizens took to the streets in May 2020.

I've been conducting diversity and cultural competency training spanning three decades.

The need for such training rears its head every few years. Social, cultural, and political tensions brought about one of those cycles during the 2016 Presidential election and continued through the COVID-19 pandemic.

Is there a will among cohousing community residents to become more culturally competent?

Be culturally competent: Do you remember the climax of *The Wizard of Oz* (1939) when Dorothy gets herself back to Kansas? Good Witch of the North, Glinda lets Dorothy in on the secret that she's always had the means to return home.

We all are capable of becoming more culturally competent by better understanding our own personality quirks.

Like Dorothy having to decide which Yellow Brick Road fork to take, evade flying monkeys, and liquidate the Wicked Witch of the West, cultural competency takes discipline and hard work by each of us to realize that we possess the inherent abilities to understand ourselves and others.

Sometimes, we need a little help from our own culturally competent Lion, Tin Man, and Scarecrow.

What is cultural competency, and why is it different from learning about diversity?

I'll provide some background.

Affirmative Action has a long history, beginning in 1961.

President Kennedy issued Executive Order (E.O.) 10925 that instructed federal contractors to take "affirmative action to ensure that applicants are treated equally without regard to race, color, religion, sex, or national origin."

That led to the Civil Rights Act, signed into law by President Johnson in 1964, that prohibited employment discrimination by any large employer.

In the current day context, following a routine arrest, George Floyd was killed by the police. That pushed covert racial injustice to the front.

Even though "All Lives Matter" during this time, "Black Lives Matter" more.

Like my neighbor, Alex, who lost his brother, Alex's family mattered more during his time of mourning. Neighbors put their interests aside, brought over covered dishes, and offered assistance, knowing that the same courtesies would be extended to them.

Lo and behold, as a result of Affirmative Action, workplaces started to include more people of color. A need then arose about how members of a once homogenous labor force needed to better understand their diverse colleagues.

That brought about "diversity training" to define the various cultures with the hope that more information meant better acceptance by the dominant white culture with no systemic changes.

Defining "diversity" became unworkable. More awareness of African Americans meant further definitions, such as Africans broken down by country and then separated by tribes and languages.

There were Africans brought to the Caribbean Islands who had a different self-identity than Africans who ended up in Brazil.

The labor force soon became integrated with Asians, and Latine which added more diversity layers.

Diversity was no longer about race but also about ethnicity. I define ethnicity as a person's place of origin. My race is Japanese, and my ethnicity is American.

The population, and subsequently the labor force, became more multicultural not only around race and ethnicity but also gender identity and sexual orientation.

Diversity training that defined and described demographics evolved into "cultural competency."

Becoming more culturally competent happens by understanding oneself and changing personal perspectives about others.

If you do a Google search, there are many iterations and definitions. For my purposes, cultural competency is an evolving process during which people recall their past experiences, reflect on them, and renew their perceptions of the world.

At any given moment, depending on past histories and experiences, individuals, groups, and communities possess various levels of cultural awareness, knowledge, and skills necessary to deal with other people.

All of our experiences are different.

"I'm color blind, and I don't see racial differences" is a comment I hear from white people.

On the surface, that statement seems socially aware. Observations like that discount everyone else's personal histories and experiences and assume that others share your worldview and don't have one of their own.

My cultural competency presentations begin with a personal voyage by remembering our histories, developmental influences, and how those experiences affect how we perceive and understand others.

Diversity, on the other hand, is descriptive of various groups. Learning all aspects of diversity is daunting since there are so many religions, languages, races, and ethnicities that the list is nearly endless.

If diversity around race, ethnicity, and gender isn't enough, add the overlays of personality types and religions that aren't limited to one population over another.

That includes extroverts/introverts, overachievers/passive, yes people/no people, Christians, Muslims, Buddhists, and all their subsets.

Because of our limited knowledge of diverse categories, judgments can lead to unintentional stereotyping.

Stereotyping is making decisions based on inaccurate or incomplete information.

When I worked for the domestic violence prevention agency, I recall a story told by one of the victim advocates who responded to a crime scene.

A bad guy had murdered an Asian woman. One of her family members began repositioning her body. A law enforcement officer was on the scene and tried to restrain the family member's actions.

The advocate intervened. She wasn't aware of the exact race and ethnicity of the victim but instinctively knew that spiritual practices are different from culture to culture and surmised that moving the body was likely part of a ritual.

That was explained to the officer who allowed the ritual to take place after the crime scene photos were taken.

Participants in my workshops, at a minimum, begin to realize that it is possible to change behaviors, recognize privilege, and understand the need to make personal sacrifices for the good of the whole.

I attended a workplace diversification workshop as a member of the Boulder Human Relations Commission. A ball-bearing factory was having difficulty keeping employees because of the constant noise. Soundproof ear covers weren't effective. Managers became aware of a nonprofit that served people who couldn't hear very well and offered to train workers.

Noise was no longer a factor that hindered employees, and the workforce stabilized.

Becoming aware of people who are different from ourselves broadens our community vision.

The process can take time and be complicated. You may lose friends but make better ones.

If you desire to live with people different than yourself in a lower-cost cohousing community, be willing to change your worldview.

"There's no place like home."

Integrate inclusion: Generally, among the audiences I've trained, every person intellectually understood the importance of diversity and inclusion but was less knowledgeable about how to make the necessary personal and culturally competent changes.

Cultural competency work can be intimate and personal. You may want to ease into it when your recruits are more comfortable with one another.

The burning souls may want to "test the water" and take some training or at least read up on the topic beforehand.

There are diversity and cultural competency trainers probably in your city or town.

Becoming more culturally competent is hard work.

Recognizing our socialization process, unpacking bias, and other learned behaviors about gender roles and racial and ethnic oppression doesn't happen overnight.

Replaying personal stories and editing them in our heads is daunting, considering Superman's American Way has been pounded into our heads since we popped out of the womb.

The simple answer is to hire a consultant to help infuse cultural competency into the community's day-to-day tasks and governance structure.

Cultural competency as an "add-on" generally means more retreats and paid experts who return to remind the community about how they've backslid.

Cohousing communities are operated and maintained by the residents who join teams to manage the Common House and maintain the common open space and finances.

Teams can integrate cultural competency into their day-to-day social fabric.

What are some ways that could play out?

For example, the SSV Common House Team purchased a set of lighter-weight dishes for some residents who had trouble managing the heavy restaurant-grade bowls and plates.

I was doing a load of laundry this morning and was reminded of when one resident reported an unexplained illness. She had an allergy to scented clothes dryer sheets. The community dryer vented from the basement, and the prevailing winds carried the chemicals into her house.

SSV decided to ban the use of odorous dryer sheets and fabric softeners. When we reduced the allergens in the laundry room, which polluted the outside air, it benefited all residents and the broader neighborhood.

The CET altered existing topics for discussion by adding culturally competent content rather than scheduling additional Sharing Circles.

The first program happened to be a talk-back with me about a documentary I made called *Beyond Heart Mountain* (2020), based on the book of the same title about my upbringing in Wyoming as a Japanese American Baby Boomer following World War II.

When I visit with forming community members or present at CohoUS conferences, I ask attendees to have honest discussions about what influenced their views about living with diverse strangers and their positive and negative personalities.

We discuss ways shared values around differences can be implemented as opposed to remaining hollow words on a piece of paper.

Integrating cultural competency into the community's social structure, if carried out efficiently, inclusion happens organically without a "program," additional training, or more meetings.

In my experience, settling into any neighborhood is stressful enough. Add onto that, jumping into daunting discussions about views around Superman's American Way that include perspectives about money, race, class, gender identity, and sexual preference.

Cultural competency makes for a more friendly environment, mostly on the governance level, when discussing HOA fees and decisions about when individual "rights" end and the community "good" begins.

Another cohousing joke is, "The best things about living in a community are the neighbors, and the worst things about community living are the neighbors."

Don't get me wrong.

Managing a cohousing community may be time-consuming, but sitting in meetings is offset by tremendous neighborly support if you need a ride to the store or help moving furniture, or if you're ill, someone will drop by with a container of hot soup.

We have community meals twice a week. I organized one around a hearty pot of "Stone Soup."

The basis of my recipe is a European folk tale about a group of weary travelers roaming through a village.

The wandering strangers scare off the residents who hide out in their homes.

The vagabonds are hungry and come up with an idea.

They find a cauldron, fill it from a nearby river, and light a fire under it. When the water boils, one traveler picks up a stone and tosses it into the pot.

"This Stone Soup would be better if we had a few vegetables," he announces.

The villagers drop their guard and open their windows and doors. They bring out their leftovers and toss them in the pot.

Soon, the village denizens shared a meal they prepared together with the travelers and celebrated their new friendships.

I put out the word that my Stone Soup would taste better if I had a few more ingredients.

Before I knew it, vegetables of all sorts spontaneously generated on the back porch table and in the Common House refrigerator.

The pot of Stone Soup simmered on the stove all day and was done in time for the community dinner that night.

My Stone Soup's secret ingredient is a smooth piece of petrified wood that my Grandfather Sakata displayed beside the felt ink blotter on his desk.

Before ballpoint pens became common, fountain pens dispensed wet ink when writing. My grandfather rolled the blotter over signatures and text to absorb excess ink.

Grandfather was a section foreman for the Chicago, Burlington & Quincy. He collected the stone from the gravel bed between the railroad tracks.

Friendships form, and informal barbecues and stone soup meals happen at the spur of the moment in cohousing communities. The SSV community plans formal events around patriotic holidays, like the red (strawberries), white (whipped cream), and blue (blueberries) pancake breakfast on July 4th.

We organize periodic "NextGen" picnics that include resident extended family members so the community can get to know future heirs and assigns should a health emergency arise.

Our SSV celebrations reinvent Superman's American Way by celebrating winter holidays, not only the Christian-based ones, including Hanukkah.

There's nothing inherently wrong with Superman's American Way, but in the context of living in a collaborative community, learning how to change personal orientation requires intentionality.

Regardless of your housing configuration, you can pour the cohousing secret sauce over your neighborhood.

While my cohousing living experience hasn't been perfect, the intentionality brings neighbors together to work through challenging large and small issues.

The upshot? If there's a community configuration that enables conversation among divergent opinions, it's cohousing.

It takes individual effort to understand the perspectives of others.

The hardest part for me is to think back and reflect on my past experiences, then change my behavior moving forward.

Social change through cohousing is a steep climb constrained by American social/cultural norms like pulling ourselves up by our bootstraps, working, climbing to the top, and trying to be neighborly from that position.

Community founding members should discuss why cultural norms create roadblocks to moving caring and interactive communities beyond what is familiar.

The founding members are the only group to fully self-select who will be in the community. After that, communities are constrained by fair housing laws that generally preclude hand-picking members.

Communities can provide information to prospective buyers about HOA membership expectations. For example, in addition to the basic cohousing expectations around consensus and participation, if a particular spiritual path is the community's higher purpose, they can explain how the various religious ceremonies are celebrated and any diet restrictions so that potential members can make a choice as to whether they would be a good fit.

Their shared values set the cultural bar for the community as it evolves into the future.

People may intellectually "value diversity," but diversity doesn't always play out, considering the typical cohouser is white, educated, high-income, high-perceived social class, and 70 percent of the time, a woman.

Being Japanese-American, I'm a cohousing outlier.

If valuing diversity is a shared value, forming community members should discuss what they would be willing to give up attitudinally and financially to include diverse members.

In one of my training sessions, I met people from a forming community who were discussing inclusion.

They decided to take some of the capital gains from their home sales to buy down housing prices in their forming community to make them more cost-efficient.

In my workshops, attendees practice ways to look at their personal histories and make changes to become more inclusive instead of only believing inclusivity is a good idea.

Personal introspection doesn't end once all the houses are constructed, and residents unpack their boxes.

Over time, the community evolves, and residents need to keep unpacking their personal histories and values as families move, people pass away, and new neighbors arrive.

Cultural competency brokers: Potential cohousers also live in gentrifying and distressed areas, in addition to the typical rural and suburban cohouser habitats.

Culturally competent developers use brokers to expand their markets by finding more accessible outreach paths into diverse communities.

It's difficult for white people to reach out directly to diverse communities. I find myself in the cultural broker role to make introductions among people wanting to meet others in communities other than their own.

Nonprofit organizations and local governments invite me to be part of boards and committees.

I wonder if they're considering me because I don't look mainstream or because I know something about the organization and its work.

"I was just contacted by a white guy who wants to meet," my friend Daniel said to me over the phone. He's the guy I was with when he was stopped in his van driving while brown.

"What does he want?" I asked.

"He wants to meet and learn about what it's like being a minority," Daniel responded incredulously. "Can you meet to talk about this? I don't know what to make of it."

Daniel and I discussed the request and agreed to meet with the curious fellow. It turned out that he was seeking cultural brokers to introduce him to diverse groups.

He rightly perceived that if he were to make direct contact, it would appear like he was seeking to involve people of color as "tokens."

As a cultural broker myself, I'm always more than happy to introduce white people to diverse organizations or groups.

If a forming cohousing community has a shared value of diversity and inclusion, I think meeting such groups on their turf is essential.

Work with the cultural broker to develop ways to make the introductions. There may be a meal or two involved.

The meetings may happen at unexpected locations, like at a place of business in an unfamiliar neighborhood.

Diverse community opinion leaders may be the assistant manager at the local *bodega* or the youth director at a church.

The effort will likely push you and your group into uncomfortable zones.

There are simple steps you can take the moment you put down this book and get on the path of becoming more culturally competent.

- Who do you sit next to in church? Sit next to a stranger.
- Who do you call to go out for coffee? Ask someone you've wanted to get to know better.
- Do you stand up as an ally? Take a risk when you hear offensive comments in the grocery store line.

Social justice marches and political elections may be personal inciting incidents that bring people together.

Whether or not you have the guts to take on the difficult task of becoming more culturally competent, it's when individuals collaborate and alter their behaviors that build bridges that close social and cultural divides, one person and one community at a time.

C'mon, I dare you.

Cohousing and Social Change: As soon as practical, I suggest the community write a story that includes your shared values.

A one-sentence premise focuses your energy on recruiting the people who are, at first blush, compatible with your proposed community.

Your story about shared values also sets the social boundaries and norms around civility and the balance between the individual's rights and the good of the whole.

What's been on my mind lately is how intentional communities can help bridge socioeconomic divides through their shared values.

Over the years, I have learned that my influence is pretty much confined to myself, the communities, and the organizations closest to me.

Rather than sitting back and watching, I prefer to be a part of the action. I was 15 when my activist efficacy began to develop.

Besides collaborative living arrangements, my early engagement in politics fit well with my first career path in public service and later negotiating my way around a cohousing community.

In May 1968, my friend Mike and I made a big cardboard sign and hauled it to a Robert Kennedy rally in Cheyenne.

That was my first exposure to a rock star politician. He signed an autograph for me, which I still have in my collection. A month later, he was shot and killed in Los Angeles.

Being from Wyoming, my early influences were Republican. I'm still atoning for my first presidential vote for Richard Nixon in 1972, but I digress.

In that vein, after the tumultuous 2016 presidential election, I wanted to make last-minute plans to check out the Women's March in Washington, D.C., that followed Inauguration Day on January 21, 2017.

I facebooked East Coast friends and colleagues, but their basements and couches were spoken for by others making the trek.

I had friends and neighbors who attended the main D.C. event and other marches around the country and resigned to sitting this one out.

Meanwhile, a friend and colleague named Marc, who, at the time, directed a Laramie, Wyoming-based activist organization, asked if I would document Women's Marchers heading to nearby Cheyenne, my hometown.

I make documentary movies, mostly about social change topics.

The early morning drive from Boulder to Laramie was uneventful. I hopped on a charter bus by the old high school was packed with mostly women, their allies, and a bunch of signs and placards.

We rumbled over Sherman Hill to Cheyenne, where we unloaded at the head of the parade by the former Union Pacific railroad depot.

According to the march organizers on their social media pages, an estimated 2,000 people trekked north on Capitol Avenue to the Wyoming Supreme Court Building lawn.

Not a big crowd compared to metropolitan urban area standards, but for a city of 60,000 locals, a couple of thousand was a huge turnout.

It was surprising to see and visit with friends who turned out on a warmish and sunny winter day, some long lost from childhood, some not so much, mostly colleagues.

We shared insights about social oppression, which is the last thing I expected to be talking about with high school classmates.

Noting that social change efforts are happening in a conservative place like Wyoming, it was then I decided to use what little influence I have to bridge socioeconomic divides and to do so through cohousing.

Since the first one in Cheyenne, I've marched in Indianapolis, Indiana (2018), Fort Washakie, Wyoming (2019), and Lander, Wyoming (2020).

I was notified about a virtual march on Washington through a COVID-distanced Zoom room in 2021. I don't think it happened.

After living at SSV for a few years, I'm convinced that intentional communities, including cohousing, are one way to help bridge cultural and socio-economic divides one community at a time.

SSV doesn't have a community theme, or higher purpose. I think nothing was consented upon largely because one of the residents is an atheist, and any reference to "higher" wasn't secular enough.

Before community dinner, someone rings a bell, calling us to order. That practice was taboo for a while when the same atheist objected. One of the more cavalier members started to ring the bell, anyway.

Some of my neighbors dub our SSV senior cohousing community a "grand social experiment."

I suppose part of that has to do with convincing older people set in their ways to work together while trying to get along with each other.

At least in my mind, the biggest challenge is balancing diverse socioeconomic perspectives, considering the typical cohouser demographics.

The SSV community is intentionally diverse in terms of material wealth and related world views around the value of money.

When it comes to agreeing on a set of shared values, there is a subtle aura around various aspects of social and economic "privilege."

Keep in mind that when forming a new or joining an existing community, it's essential to have open discussions about how your prospective members were socialized into their versions of Superman's American Way.

Despite a resident's intellectual understanding of inclusion and diversity, that sometimes doesn't match up with actions based on their backgrounds.

I only know how that has affected me. Being a Japanese-American, I'm a raisin in the Cohousing Nation oatmeal.

On top of that, I live in a lower-priced house. Being brown and poor isn't the best combination from a stereotypical perspective.

My interaction with the neighbors while breaking into the SSV community wasn't easy, particularly since I didn't know much about cohousing in the first place.

At least in my case, there wasn't much of an orientation process for new people.

Nobody introduced me to two people for several months. I'm an introvert, and eventually, I mustered up the courage to introduce myself.

One guy I never met because he was homebound, then eventually moved to a long-term care facility. The other didn't get out much.

The orientation process has improved since then. Now, when an owner sells, there is a liaison between the seller and the HOA. We've always required "serious" parties to attend a potluck dinner, a community meeting, and sit through an orientation about cohousing in the context of SSV.

Being the only brown-skin at SSV, I didn't know if that had anything to do with me left to my own devices, but it went through my mind.

I grew up as a Baby Boomer under the post-World War II anti-Asian umbrella.

My grandfather and uncle were in the wrong place at the wrong time and detained in California shortly after President Roosevelt signed Executive Order 9066 following the bombing of Pearl Harbor on December 7, 1941.

That action enabled the U.S. Army to round up 120,000 Japanese people, mainly on the West Coast.

After the U.S. Army sorted out the detainees at one of 15 assembly centers, they were transported by train to one of 10 war relocation camps in the United States interior.

Auntie Elsie was able to get her dad and brother released back to middle-of-nowhere Wyoming.

Even though my family was sequestered in Wyoming and not banished to one of the relocation camps, my family experienced overt and covert prejudice.

Later, during the 1950s, my parents visited Elsie while she was going to college in Boston. The three weren't allowed into Canada due to sedition laws that excluded Asians from crossing the border.

By the time I moved into SSV, a couple of years had passed since the community was completed and occupied.

The founding group self-selected themselves and was in the swing of things, which was good and bad.

It was good in that we didn't have to be involved with the organizational nuts-and-bolts furniture-selection phase.

It was bad because the community was in a rhythm and not open to new voices and ideas.

Since I'm usually one to jump right in and roll up my sleeves, it was pretty clear that my newbie role was to sit back and watch.

When I first moved in, SSV reminded me of a private club. The expectation was just to follow along and not ask about why things happened the way they did.

In one case, I didn't feel welcome. I remember joining a team, and a member wanted to know my credentials and if I had enough experience and knowledge. I soon quit that group.

In retrospect, I should have stuck with it, but having to continually challenge the guy and his dismissive micro-aggressions wasn't worth the brain damage.

I've always been one of the younger members at SSV. Because of my socialization, I didn't make many waves.

I don't know about others, but there's a family hierarchy around respecting elders in the Japanese culture.

There have been SSV residents old enough to be my parents. It was unnatural for me to refer to them by their first names and not Mr. or Mrs. So-and-So.

I participated at the minimum level for several years and waited on the sidelines until it was my turn.

My time to step up is beginning with all the community turnover over the past few years. I anticipate there will be significant changes around here within the near future.

A house is a house, but the community part is an entirely different overlay compared to the traditional subdivision structure where neighbors can choose to stick to themselves, paint their garage any color they want, and otherwise bowl alone.

Community members intellectually want inclusion, but they don't necessarily understand what that means emotionally, which complicates the social culture.

My across-the-sidewalk neighbor, Jim, who picked me up from the hospital in 2013, developed SSV through his company.

Boulder Housing Partners, the city housing authority, provided cheap land to developers in exchange for 40 percent deed-restricted, lower-cost homes.

The SSV community met that mark and includes six condos based on the city of Boulder's lower-priced housing program and 10 market-priced condos.

Some of the SSV market rate homeowners say they subsidize the smaller units. What actually happened was the low cost of land resulted in a greater profit margin when the big houses were sold.

Even though Diana and I sold a one-bedroom, 600 sq ft market-rate home that was appreciated by a third, we qualified for the local government's housing program and paid cash for our two-bedroom, 800 sq ft condo.

We upsized.

The City of Boulder program was originally set up for first-time home buyers. The idea was to assist with the purchase of a starter home that would later be sold when the first owner would upgrade, opening the starter home for another first time owner.

The cost of housing in Boulder has always been high. Diana and I would not be able to buy a similar home if we sold our deed-restricted SSV condo. This is likely our last place.

Seventy percent of SSV houses have changed hands. Some places more than once. It's no surprise that the lowest turnover rate is among the cost-efficient condos.

We're not the only owners who tie up the lower-priced housing stock long-term. The city is constantly having to acquire or build cost-efficient owner-occupied homes or rental apartments since there is little turnover.

I'm reminded about my frat bro, Tom, who's lived in the same rent-controlled apartment in New York City for the past 40 years.

We soon learned what it's like to be "one of those" owners of a government-subsidized, cheap house.

Cohousing affordability is a conundrum for most forming communities, particularly since smaller and lower-priced homes are likely fewer compared to the number of expensive ones.

While spoken and unspoken, those with the larger and most expensive homes have large amounts of money tied up in their real estate.

As such, owners of large houses want to fund the capital repair and replacement funds to as high a level as practical to protect their investments.

Those of us in smaller deed-restricted homes that slowly appreciate have less incentive to pay higher HOA reserve fund fees. Our homes are worth the same, but rather than having our assets up in a house, we can deploy our investments and savings with more flexibility.

Regardless, I don't mind paying into the reserve fund. I've heard of HOAs that have underfunded their replacement fund. The monthly due amounts may be low in the short term, but hefty special assessments can be catastrophic for those owners who haven't set aside savings for that possibility.

The SSV HOA requires its members to carry

I, for one, place a higher value on the social aspects of the community. That's difficult when discussions about finances dominate that.

We have a well-funded reserve account to pay for capital replacements like the elevator or roof as they deteriorate over the years. The "unseen" infrastructure, like water, sewer, and electricity within the walls and other common spaces, like the irrigation system, will also need replacement in another 20 or 30 years.

"Those pipes and wires will never have to be replaced," is the fallback answer. The HOA is planning to schedule a community discussion about whether this is an issue we need to worry about.

Having bought and sold two market-rate condos before SSV, Diana and I soon found that living in a house governed by a different set of rules was a big eye-opener.

Not only is our property deed restricted, the city of Boulder owns a small percentage. We have to ask permission if we want to make an improvement like buying new floor coverings. If the City approves the expenditure, the price can be added to the sales price.

I've developed lower-priced and cost-efficient housing in my various past lives and am now participating as a recipient in a local government housing program.

I was aware of stereotypes about people who reside in "low-income" housing.

Since I now live in a government-sponsored small and lower-cost home, I've become more personally aware of the oppressive language that goes along with the stereotypes that include terms like "charity cases," "think different," "lower class," "no pride," "don't fit in," etc.

The speakers of those derogatory terms exhibit their long-held attitudes that are difficult to reverse, even for the most progressive and socially aware person who has taken cultural competency training.

Undoing oppressive and dismissive attitudes takes time, work, and practice.

Over the years, I've learned how to push a few buttons to make a point and intentionally create learning moments.

I've spent quite a lot of time thinking up "snappy answers to stupid questions."

I was sitting in an emergency row exit seat. If there's a crash landing, that's the row where passengers have to spring to action and open the hatch.

"CAN - YOU - SPEAK - ENGLISH ! ! !" a flight attendant slowly annunciated and stared at me so I could see her lips moving.

"I'm Japanese, not deaf," was my smarty pants response.

Another time, I was waiting for assistance at the local camera store counter.

"Can you read this?" A woman tapped me on the shoulder and held up an instruction manual with the page turned to an Asian language. "No, I'm sorry, but I don't understand Spanish."

For context, a cohousing community consists of individuals and families living in privately occupied homes with shared common spaces.

Everyone lives independently but shares in maintaining their community by helping out in the garden, managing social events, keeping track of the finances, etc.

Regardless of the political or social labels, the national mood at any moment in time amplifies how individuals deal with their perceptions about differences among people.

For Baby Boomers and older, those experiences span from World War II anti-Japanese sentiments, U.S. segregation, and separate but equal "Jim Crow" laws to Muslim xenophobia following 9/11.

Who was Jim Crow?

He wasn't a real person. A white actor named Thomas Dartmouth Rice in New York City performed in blackface and wore shabby, tattered clothes.

His actions exaggerated the stereotypical slow-moving, slow-talking demeanor of lazy enslaved people he claimed to have observed. His racist "song and dance" act was called *Jump, Jim Crow*.

His schtick was popular in New York, where blackface minstrel shows became a common form of musical theater.

Jim Crow became associated with legalized racial segregation.

Personal understanding of protected classes of race, gender identity, sexual orientation, and physical ability is objectively grounded.

Perceptions of social and economic overlays to each class are more subjective.

Communities and their members that intentionally align the objective and subjective views of protected classes can better unpack their self-perceptions of privilege.

Unpacking that baggage is hard work. Apparent mistakes, stepping on toes, and other "on-the-job" training experiences can cause hard feelings.

If your community has a shared value that corrections shouldn't be taken personally but rather viewed as learning moments, then anger and disappointment can be repositioned as positive outcomes.

Shaking our self-interests is a difficult task because Superman's American Way is ingrained into our collective psyche.

My suggestion for community members, particularly those in the forming stages, is to get to know your potential neighbors more than on a superficial level.

"Oh, I like to go on hikes," or "That's great that you're an avid reader, I am too," or "I like to watch old movies" are some high-level icebreakers.

The point is that everyone likes to do broad brush activities, including my examples.

It's easy to get to know WHAT a person is about but challenging to understand WHO they are.

What's more important is finding out who the chronic overachievers, the control freaks, and the overly competitive or mega-cooperative people are.

"Where did you live before your current location, and what type of house do you live in now?" is an icebreaker I like to use when facilitating meetings with cohousers or prospective cohousers.

If you're thinking about plopping down your life savings to buy a house in a community with a bunch of strangers, you should at least go into it with knowledge about the quirks your potential neighbors may hold.

My icebreaker gets people to talk a bit about their histories, at least as far back as the last place where they lived.

If you ask about their job, the likelihood of a rich discussion is low since the frame of reference is small.

Suppose a person says they currently live in a rental apartment or a condominium complex.

In that case, I surmise that they have experience living close to others, including tolerating noise from upstairs and possibly being more respectful of others in small ways.

That was my experience. I grew up with a huge extended family, lived in the dorms in college, my first house was a co-op with two other guys, and in an apartment above a hardware store and an intentional Buddhist community.

Since those early years, I've chosen to be an urban rat. Living in cohousing suited me well.

On the other hand, if a person says they live in a 4,000 sq ft prairie palace on 10 acres, that would tell me that they haven't had to ask anyone whether or not they can plant a tree over here or chop one down over there.

Since few neighbors are nearby, living in isolation would be a big transition to living on top of others in a high-density condominium complex.

Early on in the "getting to know you" phase, asking about transitions from an individualized lifestyle to a collective one can be revealing.

Maybe you'll end up with community members who all have had that single-family lifestyle experience.

A question I asked a few of my neighbors for my *Aging Gratefully* documentary was if they had any tips for others developing cohousing communities.

One guy identified the elephant in the Common House.

"Have residents of similar means," he said of income disparities between the market rate homeowners and those of us in the lower-priced condos. "You can build with Mercedes Benz parts or Chevy parts. When it comes to replacement, Mercedes is more expensive. Maybe you should have started out with Chevy parts in the first place."

I thought about making up a scenario but decided that using a "real-world" example would be more helpful.

The community went through a year-long evaluation of the HOA due structure. It was a very collaborative "Bubbles and Boxes" approach.

All the residents worked closely together and shared their views about the outcome. Despite divergent mixed ideas, a consensus was reached on a difficult issue.

The cats were successfully herded.

SSV cohousing consists of 16 condos. Ten are worth, on average, $1,000,000. Compare that to the remaining six included in the city of Boulder housing program valued at around $200,000.

The big homes are not only more expensive but triple in size as the cost-efficient condos.

When I first moved into SSV, the first thing that I noticed was the high level of attention paid to individual needs.

Because most community members own big homes, decision-making was collaborative but to the benefit of the larger condo owners who had more voices.

That continues today, with the smaller units asked to subsidize the larger units' HOA due assessments.

Many HOAs determine their fees based on square footage. What a massive condo owner would pay would be incredibly high in communities with vast differences in home square footage, like SSV.

A complex calculation in the context of equality divides up expenses related to the shared spaces and Common House.

Because of the theoretical cohousing tenet that all owners are equal in status, the 800 and 3,000 sq ft units pay one-sixteenth of the common space operation and maintenance costs.

In practice, the funding formula flattens out the due amounts, with smaller units paying disproportionately more, similar to the regressive U.S. income tax structure.

The SSV due structure is an example of how the few gave up more to subsidize the many.

As my neighbor points out in the *Aging Gratefully* documentary, cohousing communities should consist of homes roughly the same size and value, so when the individual HOA due schedule is determined, the bottom lines are similar.

If income diversity is essential to you, think about a community with a majority of lower-priced condo owners. That significant action demonstrates how the dominant culture can cede power and reinvent Superman's American Way.

Attract the community members you want: I firmly believe that if a community advocate comes up with a compelling story about the group's mission and values, it will narrow the people who want to join you.

The first step of my book writing workflow is developing a short pitch that conveys the basic story idea to others.

I've adapted pitch writing for forming a cohousing community.

There are plenty of cohousing war stories out there about communities that have a hard time keeping a group of people together.

Forming communities go through many people over time. Coho Stout communities take years to complete. Some people drop out because they can't wait.

At least keep your prospective members interested with a community story.

Ernest Hemingway says to write "one true sentence." To get started, I'm talking literally about writing one sentence boiling down millions of dollars and several years to 140 characters, basically a tweet.

It's your elevator speech. You know, shortening your story into one sentence you can recite to someone in the length of time it takes for you both to get on the elevator and depart on the next floor.

Plus, you'll also need something to talk about at your next cocktail party.

Write your community story: Your story is important because you're trying to attract people to join your community.

"What's happening with your cohousing community?" I'll ask during a break at a conference.

"We're having problems. Oh, we had an architect, but he quit us. Then we had five people drop out because they couldn't wait any longer, and we lost the option on our property," is a usual response I'll hear as I wander away to look at the T-shirts for sale.

You lost me at "We're having problems," and I'm back to the appetizer table for another plate of hummus and celery.

I would rather learn from you where your community is located, whether you're multigenerational or senior, and about your community's "higher purpose."

I can guarantee you that if you have a community story about anything other than your problems, the conversation, at least with me, will be more engaging.

I'll deconstruct the first pitch line I gave for a Lite project proposed in Colorado Springs, Colorado.

What's the fundamental truth about storytelling? Stories are finite. There's a beginning, middle, and end.

That's it. Within that three-act structure, a true story sentence includes the project proponents (Who), their goal (What), and their challenge (Why).

Who - There's no need to name the proponents. Names have no intrinsic information and are useless words. Instead, tell us something about the story.

> *A few gentle-on-the-earth burning souls dedicated to a healthy lifestyle ...*

What - Clearly present the main goal that drives your story.

> *A few gentle-on-the-earth burning souls dedicated to a healthy lifestyle create a community by repurposing a vacant big-box commercial property to build a new neighborhood ...*

Why - Describe the Challenge as a "What if" statement and add the challenges.

> *What if a few-gentle-on-the-earth burning souls create a community by repurposing a vacant big-box commercial property to build a new neighborhood by attracting 48 creative thinkers to live in a like-minded cohousing community?*

In one true sentence, I created a desire among a specific group of people. The story has a complete arc, as well as what happens in between.

This version is for zoning officials, to obtain grants and is written with a little too much jargon.

For presentations to the public, I would tweak it by rewriting it to be more conversational, depending on the audience.

Your sentence should be a principled message as opposed to a jargon-laced one. Here are a couple of message examples. This is particularly important if you live in a socially conservative community.

- **Principled message** - The development is energy and time-efficient.
- **Jargony version** - The sustainable development nullifies climate change and provides weekly community meals.
- **Jargony perception** - anti-business and industry, over-regulation, loss of individual liberty.

- **Principled message** - This development is about strong family values that provide a safe place to raise kids in a cohesive neighborhood with excellent schools.
- **Jargony version** - This development is about marriage equality, affordable housing, viable community policing, and low student-teacher ratios.

- **Jargony perception** - pro-gay; handouts to poor; gun control; pro-teacher unions

Even if you set up a table at the farmers' market to take names of interested people, you're not looking for 1,000 or 500 people. You're likely looking for likely around 150 members or less. In the next chapter, I'll discuss the basis of this number.

It sounds contrived and rehearsed, which it is. It's like when you learn conversational Spanish while laid over at the airport before heading out to the beaches of Mazatlán.

Not only do you need to know the phrases, but you also need to know the context, when to say them, and how to respond.

It's the same with your story premise. Practice so it becomes a part of your language set.

Get it in your head, ready to spit it out when there's a lull in the conversation or there's a good segue when other party-goers circulate around to you.

Stories are never perfect and dynamic. I know this to be true because I wake up a different person every day.

That means I have to keep testing out all my story premises as my life changes.

Every word counts. Getting the delivery right takes constant word fiddling. Fiddle and test, fiddle and test, and then fiddle some more.

You should feel like Itzhak Perlman practicing both parts of the *Double Violin Concerto in D Minor* by J.S. Bach.

Share your story: Now that you've thought through your community story based on your values, how do you find people to join?

A few terms get tossed around and confused when it comes to outreach to the broader public. To be consistent, these are the terms and definitions I use.

"Publics" is a term I learned as a public relations intern during graduate school. A "public" is a group of individuals that shares some commonality, similar to economic markets.

The "publics," in aggregate, make up the "general public," similar to the "mass market."

The approach I use is a combination of Marketing and Public Relations (MPR).

What is marketing? In the context of cohousing, marketing is the process that identifies markets of people that share similar demographic or consumptive characteristics.

The mass market consists of people who live in houses.

You can break down the housing market into smaller markets, including owners, renters, seniors, families, etc.

The housing sub-markets can be further differentiated based on high income, low income, race and ethnicity, gender identity, sexual orientation, etc.

After you identify your markets, craft messages that resonate with each, the message is the same, but terminology and contexts are market-specific.

This is where you can apply your one true pitch.

If you're writing a message to seniors, use Beatles music and references to President Kennedy. A message to a Millennial may be around Lizzo music and YouTube product influencers.

Getting your messages purveyed precisely how you want them is "unearned media," which is purchased advertising. Paid advertising allows you to tell your story exactly how you want.

Effective news releases gain "earned media" results that may end up as a story in the newspaper, radio, TV, or some other media forms like a blog or podcast.

There's no telling when or if your story will see the light of day. That leads me to public relations.

What is 'Public Relations' (PR)? PR is the primary means of generating "earned media," which is nurturing a positive perspective about your community to your identified publics or markets.

The media forms you use to get your messages across are the same for market development and include traditional sources like TV, newspapers, and radio; social media including blogs, emails, and podcasts; and in-person meetings like speakers' bureaus and guest appearances on radio shows.

Write your news release with specific story angles. The likelihood of a unique story getting ink or airtime is greater than a generic meeting notice.

If it's a slow news day, the TV station or newspaper may send a reporter.

Start out with a general "you're invited to our cohousing meeting" news release that may get tossed into the trash basket. Create an action about a local person or topic.

Then, start getting specific with a news story about a community dinner. The Lifestyle editor may end up writing a piece about that in the food section.

The Real Estate editor may cover a story about your cohousing community, the first in the county.

Always write messages so they wrap around your community story pitch about attracting members.

The Features editor might want a positive pandemic story. For example, an excellent human-interest story activity happened at the Wild Sage Cohousing in Boulder.

The community across the street from SSV sewed masks in the Common House for frontline emergency responders during COVID-19 isolation.

I offer up my *Aging Gratefully* cohousing movies to forming communities. A screening adds content to organizational meetings.

In the case of a movie screening, notify the Entertainment Editor at your local paper that you're showing a great film over at the library.

Targeted messages build mutually beneficial relationships between cohousing communities, their publics, and markets.

MPR messaging: Forming communities likely have limited budgets and rely on low/no budget earned income public relations activities to get out the word about new member recruitment. I use a four-step approach called RACE.

- **Research** your story and use your community story premise to develop your markets and publics. Who - are potential people to contact? Where - is the geographic area where you want to recruit?

- **Actions** should be developed that are useful and credible. Include your burning soul members as speakers, cohousing film screenings, partnerships with organizations that share your philosophy, and collaborate with cultural brokers if you want to connect with diverse publics and markets.

- **Communication** objectives should be strategized, resulting in messages that are understandable to each identified market or public. Communications are through earned and unearned (if you have a budget) traditional media coverage and nontraditional media such as social media.

- **Evaluation** determines if your actions were effective and explained effectively to each identified public or market. Evaluation tools can be as simple as counting the number of attendees and a talk-back at the end of an event. Conduct more formal surveys using printed forms or online platforms like surveymonkey.com or customized Google forms. These data circle back and inform the Research step to improve future actions and communication.

Most cohousing communities have a shared value of inclusion and diversity.

Diverse markets and publics are difficult for typical predominantly Caucasian cohousing communities to reach.

3c. Engage – Dunbar's Number

Cohousing neighbors commit to being part of a community for mutual benefit. Cohousing engages its community members to develop a culture of sharing and caring.

What is the ideal community size?

Anthropologist Robin Dunbar proposed a theory suggesting that each of us can effectively manage no more than 150 people and maintain genuine interpersonal connections by juggling friendships, keeping track of birthdays, and sharing day-to-day updates.

Dunbar's Number was derived from analyzing the relationship between brain size and social group size in primates and applying it to humans.

Exceeding 150 makes it challenging to maintain solid and cohesive bonds that would otherwise require stricter social rules around implementing community values for larger groups. Those efforts would likely include mandatory meetings and activities to ensure interpersonal interactions.

This "sweet spot" fosters a strong sense of community, facilitating meaningful social interactions.

My anecdotal observation is that 32 households or around 80 residents are the ideal cohousing community sizes. SSV is smaller than most, with 16 condos occupied by 28 residents.

Size is also a negative because there are fewer people to do the work. That's problematic as residents age, and their abilities diminish.

Closely associated with shared values are community relationships. Both overlap with community participation. Having fewer people in a senior community has its plusses and minuses.

The main benefit is familiarity with neighbors happens more organically since people randomly bump into each other. Common meals are smaller even when there is high attendance.

The SSV dinners average between 40 and 50 percent. The number of diners increases if a topic is to be discussed or a special program is offered and it's summer.

As a practice, the SSV Community Enhancement Team (CET) convenes periodic Sharing Circles when members get together and share what's been happening in their lives.

The Circles are well attended because the SSV population usually has 20 or more members joining the conversations.

A resident recently died. SSV is altering its monthly community meeting structure by limiting business to an hour and substituting a Sharing Circle based on a topic of interest for the second hour. A grieving circle was added with a follow-up to that discussion a month later.

Cohousing is characterized as "touchy-feely" based on interpersonal activities like the SSV Sharing Circles, which are pretty well attended.

Similar sessions probably don't take place in regular neighborhoods.

Each Sharing Circle helps reinvent Superman's American Way. Based on the agreed-upon community vision and values, residents feel safe discussing personal feelings and vulnerabilities. There's no group pressure to participate.

Thirty residents are easily mobilized. The Care Network is a subset of the CET that monitors the community's well-being. Members keep their ears to the ground to learn about health issues any neighbor might have.

The Network organized a meeting with the Boulder Fire Department to explain the importance of personal information for the red vinyl File of Life holders that are stuck on refrigerator doors.

The HOA purchased an Automated External Defibrillator (AED) a few years back, but nobody knew how to use it. Shari, daughter of Jim and Brownie Leach, is an Emergency Medical Technician (EMT) who provided an AED and a Cardio-Pulmonary Resuscitation (CPR) class.

It wasn't until I was on my deathbed in 2013 that I realized the importance of my cohousing community relationships. Unseen to the casual observer was the dark business side of the healthcare system that exacerbated my illness by adding emotional stress.

After learning about some of the comments from the nurses who paid attention to me at the hospital, I'm surprised I survived, considering the administrative hassles I had keeping my health insurance coverage intact.

Anyone who disfavored the Affordable Care Act (Obamacare) when it was first approved in 2013, or now for that matter, hasn't been sick lately.

I don't think anybody has any idea about the details of their healthcare coverage. I barely did myself, other than knowing that the end of the year rolled around and I needed a new policy.

Being a self-employed schmuck, I didn't have a Human Resources office to negotiate a group plan, like when I worked real jobs.

I didn't plan on getting sick in December when all insurance policies expire.

I hadn't used up any of my high deductible. Since I didn't get sick often, for all practical purposes, I didn't have insurance.

Obamacare had its first open enrollment at the end of 2013, which further complicated things.

I probably was notified about my policy expiring but put it off. In previous years, I let the policy rollover. If the premium price went up, that triggered me to research alternatives.

The Obamacare process was theoretical, with an untested website where self-employed and poor folk, I was both, could sign up for health insurance.

Keep in mind that Obamacare is set up for very few people, something like 15 percent.

Most Americans get health insurance from an employer or another federal program like Medicare, the Veteran's Administration, Social Security, etc.

I was mentally out of it because of the painkillers. Signing up online, there was nobody I could ask for help from Mr. Frequently Asked Questions.

Eventually, I renewed my insurance by signing up for a policy through the Obamacare insurance exchange website. It was still a high-deductible policy, but the monthly premiums were less because of tax credits.

Health care reform only has to do with people like me who were flat on their backs pushing the hospital room call light, hoping a nurse's assistant would come by to empty the urinal or patch my bedsores.

For healthy people, lying in a hospital is mostly theoretical.

Previous to this, I can't remember ever using my health insurance except for an annual physical and high blood pressure medicine.

When my shit literally hit the fan, I, as well as countless other people, got caught up in the big political fight over Obamacare.

Meanwhile, even though I couldn't stand, walk, or otherwise take care of myself, the hospital kicked me out since I wasn't improving. Besides that, I was cantankerous.

A couple of EMTs lifted me and my wheelchair into the back of the ambulance. I was strapped in for the 45-minute drive to the rehabilitation place in Denver.

Not being able to move on my own, I slid out of the wheelchair and bounced around like a rag doll. I felt like the dead guy, Bernie, in that bad movie *Weekend at Bernie's* (1989).

The EMT pulled over at the cooking school on Quebec Street and repositioned me before getting to the Manor Care rehab center in Glendale, a Denver neighborhood.

The rehab center was an hour from Boulder and mainly served geriatric patients. I was the youngest one there.

A concierge-type guy checked me into the room. He handed me a booklet listing the amenities and services available, including a coupon for a haircut at the salon.

The space was lovely, like a hotel room with good light.

I had a couple of roommates while I was there. I enjoyed meeting some folks from Denver. City folks are more down-to-earth than Boulder people.

The dining room tables seemed higher than a household kitchen table. Maybe that was because the wheelchair was shorter than a regular chair.

The food was okay, but the main objective was to keep their patients alive, and that's about it.

I learned about an underground menu that offered choices prepared on the spot, like sandwiches and salads.

Those were good options when the "hot meals" weren't that tasty, which was most of the time.

Manor Care had its market nailed down. The background music was a Denver radio station that played World War II-era tunes.

I've always been an easy-listening music fan and didn't find it annoying or distracting.

Truth be told, a couple of my digital music playlists are Herb Albert and Tijuana Brass and Burt Bacharach's greatest hits.

The rehab ritual was waking up, breakfast, sitting around, rehab therapy, more sitting around, lunch, more sitting around, maybe more therapy, more sitting around, dinner, and more sitting around before going to bed.

It got a little monotonous plotting out the day based on mealtime and when *Law and Order: SVU* reruns were on TV.

Early during my treatment, I was very weak. It was a challenge to lift food from the plate to my mouth.

A terry cloth "clothes protector" was standard issue. The bib didn't tie around the neck but cut to lay over the shoulders.

The amount of food that fell off my fork surprised me. Give me a pair of chopsticks any day.

I was amazed that I received enough physical and occupational therapy after two weeks to walk out, albeit with a walker, compared to when I arrived as a total invalid.

My friend and production partner, Michael, drove to Manor Care to pick me up. When he dropped me off at the SSV loading zone, it was the last weekend in January. I was surprised about the casseroles and covered dishes that showed up from my neighbors.

I appreciated the gestures, but notified the community to bring by nonperishable items since I could only eat so many scalloped potatoes.

Some pitched in with money to defray the transportation costs Diana had to make between Boulder and the hospital.

Other than the neighborly support, the community treated me as if I hadn't been away.

That was good because I didn't want empathy or sympathy. I just wanted to be left alone during my recovery.

That Sunday was Super Bowl XLVIII between the Denver Broncos and the Seattle Seahawks.

I wheeled myself down to the Common House, managed to open the door, and bounced over the threshold to check out the action.

There were the usual Super Bowl manly snacks on the kitchen counter, like bags of various kinds of chips, salsa, Velveeta and Rotel dip.

I choked down a few nachos and a wing or two but had to cut the afternoon short at halftime because the hose dangling out of my abdomen began to leak. The seal hadn't seated itself fully.

After the ulcer patch healed up, my eating habits changed. The fabric webbing kept my abdomen from expanding. I used to take "all you can eat" as a challenge.

Having a large extended family had its benefits growing up. One negative was many babysitting choices.

My sister and I weren't allowed to join our parents at a restaurant.

These days, childcare costs double the price of dinner.

Given a choice, I liked to stay over with my maternal grandparents. They had a big front room with one of those wrap-around couches and a loveseat. There were plenty of cushions to construct forts.

I don't think my grandmother was too crazy about it, but my sister and I had fun.

Then, one night, we were granted a rite of passage.

The entire family went to Petersen's Buffet on East Lincolnway in a shopping district across the street from Holliday Park.

It was "all you can eat," and that I did. We always had enough on the dinner table, but not roast beef, fried chicken, two kinds of Jell-O salad, dessert choices, and endless milk at the same meal.

When we arrived home, I don't know if this helped, but my mom made me walk around the block several times to "settle my stomach."

Since moving to Colorado, if I get to choose a birthday bash venue, it's at a giant pink stucco building in the style of a cathedral on West Colfax in Lakewood called Casa Bonita.

During the COVID-19 pandemic, the gawdy landmark closed. It was subsequently purchased by *South Park* TV show creators Trey Parker and Matt Stone. An episode of the animated series featured Casa Bonita.

The classic restaurant reopened, but there's a huge waiting list to get a chance to dine there. Potential patrons are required to sign up online and will eventually be notified. I still haven't heard back. Maybe the newness has worn off, and anyone can go now.

The specialty back in the day was "all you can eat" Mexican food. Although the fare was more accurately described as "all you can choke down."

The typical customers were large families, birthday parties, and bus-loads of school kids. Acapulco-esque cliff divers entertained patrons.

Casa Bonita was one big theater in the round and offered performances by cowboys and bad guys, ending with the villain falling into the emerald pool water below.

Speaking of nachos, the Casa Bonita nachos were pretty good, but the main courses included endless *enchiladas* or *tacos* and the best not-too-greasy and light *sopapillas* with honey.

After my surgery, I had a birthday dinner there. That was when I realized I wouldn't be able to chow down as I did in the past.

I've heard that the food quality has improved but the prices have gone up considerably. At least I won't be tempted to overdo it and can enjoy the high-diving gorilla.

The Super Bowl wasn't much of a game, with the Broncos getting trounced 43-8 by the Seahawks.

Now in homebound rehab, I attended the Boulder International Film Festival (BIFF) over President's Day weekend as part of my occupational therapy. I'm on the BIFF Board of Directors.

It was my first "off-campus" outing since Dec. 16, 2013. Before this, I was in an ambulance, hospital, ambulance, rehab center, and back in the condo.

My faithful caregiver, Diana, wheeled me to the BIFF reception at one of the downtown hotels. Seeing the world from a wheelchair is a different view.

As an old guy, I appreciated my month-long stint, but I was unable to walk around very well.

The ramp to the hotel entrance was very steep and had a hairpin turn to negotiate. I couldn't have done that myself.

When I was ambulatory, I didn't realize that elevator wheelchair access was out of the way at best, not to mention the bumps and lumps on the floor.

I was able to get back into the editing booth. As part of my occupational therapy, I cut together a Shirley MacLaine tribute that screened Saturday night at the BIFF.

That was also good for my mental health because I felt my work still had value.

Being deathbed sick was a big wake-up call for me, particularly about big-picture issues, mainly around downsizing and relationships with people.

Small picture issues? I'm now more serious about plotting out exit strategies for projects I head up, handing off assignments to others, and getting ready to stop answering the phone and "retire."

After two months out of the hospital, I still considered myself "disabled.'

I forced myself to get out and about in the SSV neighborhood but encountered obstacles like steps, slight inclines, and places without banisters. Those barriers helped me regain arm strength, which was good.

I didn't notice accessibility issues around SSV until I had to relearn how to walk. I tried walking up the steps on the east-end sidewalk, but my legs collapsed from under me. I suggested to the Systems and Buildings Team that handrails should be added.

"Walk around the block to the other end," was the culturally incompetent solution. The team got around to making the improvement after my nonagenarian neighbors fell.

What a long, strange trip it's been and still is!

Introverts and Extroverts: I went into cohousing seclusion by cutting back on my Silver Sage Village participation level following a health scare in 2014.

You can choose as much privacy or community as you like in cohousing, and I chose more privacy. It was hard enough to regain my strength and catch up with my life, let alone deal with the meetings and think up small talk topics at potluck dinners.

That was a simple transition, considering I was out of the SSV loop for six weeks before while flat on my back in the hospital, followed by two months of in-home therapy. I didn't get out much.

Part of my self-imposed isolation was health-related, but being an introvert, dropping out came naturally and was a welcomed break from the cohousing community hubbub. I wouldn't be missed since some of the over-participators would complete whatever work I abandoned.

Why should introverts matter in cohousing?

Author Susan Cain wrote a book called *Quiet* in 2012 that gives pretty good insight into how introverts are pushed aside in an extroverted world.

She explains that extroverts solve problems spontaneously, prefer speed over accuracy, and move to another problem if frustrated or discouraged. Introverts tend to be more contemplative and accurate and think through a problem before trying to solve it.

The consensus-based and deliberate tenets of cohousing are more introverted in nature than extroverted. Statistically, 30 percent of the population self-identify as extroverts and 70 percent as introverts.

The data are sparse, but it's been estimated that introverts are overrepresented in cohousing, with 80 to 85 percent self-identifying as introverts. My theory about the disparity is that cohousing community social structures are highly organized and create an environment of forced acceptance.

Residents have all agreed to include everyone through interactions at regular meetings, sharing planned dinners, and social gatherings.

Cohousing communities try to implement flat leadership structures but still have built-in hierarchies required by outside-world government-administered Homeowner HOA regulations, like HOA officers, a board of directors, and committees with leaders.

I saw an article published in the *Harvard Business Review* that even though extroverts are in the minority, 96 percent of leaders and managers self-identify as extroverts.

The few extroverts in cohousing communities can wedge themselves into traditional leadership roles, which can cause participation conflicts among the majority of community introverts.

Each of us has complex personalities, including where we fall on the extroversion–introversion spectrum. All of us have characteristics of both.

Because of this divide, I suggest that communities, particularly those in the forming stages, get to know their potential neighbors more than on a superficial level.

"Oh, I like to go on hikes," or "That's great that you're an avid reader, I am too," or "I like to watch old movies" are some high-level icebreakers.

The point is that everyone can agree about high-level interests like hiking, reading, and watching movies. It's easy to know WHAT a person is about but more challenging to understand WHO they are.

While there are many facets to a person, determining who the introverts and extroverts are can be eye-opening.

Residents in established communities have learned their neighbors' good and bad habits through experience, and the personality exercise may be too personal, but it's worth the exercise.

If you're considering plopping down your life savings to buy a house in a community with a bunch of strangers, you should at least go into it with knowledge about the quirks your potential neighbors may hold.

They may wonder the same things about you.

A revealing and, at the same time, fun, community-building activity is for all to take a simple personality test. Take into account your members' personal safety levels if you decide to do this. Be sure that all are okay with exposing their inner selves to others.

There are many measuring tools, including the Enneagram, and True Colors. I like the Myers-Briggs test, which I've administered at a variety of workshops. At least for me, the activity is low risk. The results give insight into how individuals may react interpersonally and when making decisions.

Isabel Myers-Briggs and her mother, Katherine Cook Briggs, developed the measurement tool based on Carl G. Jung's theory of psychological types.

- Source of personal energy:
    o Extroverted (E) vs. Introverted (I)
- How information is processed:
    o Sensing (S) vs. Intuition (N)
- Decision-making process:
    o Thinking (T) vs. Feeling (F)
- How our worlds are organized:
    o Judging (J) vs. Perceiving (P)

Myers-Briggs estimates where a person fits on the introvert to extrovert continuum. I'm an INFP on the introversion spectrum.

It's a rare personality type. The Myers-Briggs interpretation says I tend to be quiet, nonjudgmental, and imaginative. I utilize a caring and creative approach in my life. All of that's true, and I can be an extrovert on demand but get stressed out when that happens.

If you're curious, there are any number of websites that offer free versions of the test and interpretations of the various personality types.

I use a free test and analyses of various personality types and combinations provided by www.16personalities.com

While the four categories are general, they provide a framework that provides insight into members of any community, be it cohousing or your book club.

How people play with others is a function of their basic personalities. When I'm writing a book, I assign my characters with Myers-Briggs personality types and how they match up with one another. This gives me insight into how the characters interact as the story moves forward.

In any community, no person is the same. We are multi-dimensional beings and possess introvert and extrovert characteristics, and our traits are not exclusive.

Cohousers mirror the wider world and span the extroversion-introversion spectrum. The cooperative synthesis of the two extremes favors tendencies of introversion.

Uber Extroverted People are more aggressive and exemplify Superman's American Way: Winning is better than losing, bigger is better than smaller, as we fight a never-ending battle for truth, justice, and the American Way.
- Take more from the community than they give back.
- Need power and control.
- Seek personal advantage to win.
- Use skills to dominate.
- Believe the loudest voice wins.
- Work alone as a rugged individual.
- Celebrate personal independence.
- Manipulate the system to benefit self-interests.

Uber Introverted People are more passive and less concerned about competition.

- Play well with other introverts.
- Give more to the community than they take.
- Give up power and control.
- Seek attention as a way to connect.
- Give away skills for no gain.
- Move immediately to a compromise position.
- Value the group over the individual.
- Rely on over-dependent relationships.
- Self-sacrifice to the point of personal harm.

Balanced Cooperative People are the synthesis. Ideal cohousers set their passive and aggressive tendencies aside.

- Collaborate with those with broad-ranging points of view.
- Seek an understanding of collective action.
- Share skills for the common good.
- Know their role as a team player.
- Balance self and community interest.
- Balance independence and over-dependence.
- Honor differences to enhance collaboration.
- Balance service to others and personal needs.

Forming and established communities can evaluate where their members fall on the personality continuum and agree ahead of time about how the two extremes can lead to a collaborative balance.

All it takes is a few Uber Extroverts to dominate and disrupt the consensus process, mainly because they will steamroll over Uber Introverts.

A few years ago, I was producing a documentary at a cohousing community. I had to cut my visit short because the community had hired an out-of-state consultant to facilitate a conflict resolution between the community and a member who refused to let loose of a project.

If you're an introvert, think about a time you were dismissed or pushed aside by an aggressor and how that made you feel. Knowing the tendencies of aggressive people, how might you have handled it differently?

If you're an extrovert, what was an incident when you exerted your aggressive approach on a passive person? How would the outcome have been different if you were more collaborative?

Here it is, 10 years after my self-imposed isolation from community participation. More of my neighbors have moved or died during that decade, and new people have joined the community.

Now that I'm no longer a newbie, I've found my voice after climbing out of my hole and have learned to hold myself and the Uber Extroverts more accountable.

Risk and Protective Factors: Risks and protective factors are related to the Uber Extrovert - Uber Introvert spectrum.

Those are two jargony terms but important concepts when maintaining order in any organization, including a cohousing community.

Protective factors are buffers against risks that contribute to disruptive behavior. I formerly worked in the positive youth development and domestic violence prevention fields.

Parts of those two jobs involved training in strength-based cultural competency. I melded that together with the cohousing secret sauce.

Risk contributes to conflicts among diverse personalities, and protective factors can buffer against risks. One vital protective factor is cultural competency.

Risk factors: They increase a person's possibility of committing disruptive or violent acts.

Like "diversity," the list of potential risk factors is nearly endless. It is possible to be disruptive or commit violent acts with or without any of the risk factors listed below.

However, the more risk factors a person is exposed to, the greater the possibility of committing disruptive or violent acts. Here's a list of risk factors possibly encountered in a cohousing community:

Personal risk factors
- Has a history of emotional outbursts.

- Resorts to name-calling.
- Exhibits bullying behavior.
- Has a history of being pushed around.
- Makes threats of violence.
- Abuses of alcohol or drugs.
- Exhibits moodiness.
- Blames others for personal problems.
- Desires power and control.
- Experienced recent humiliation, loss, or rejection.
- Maintains poor peer relations.
- Isolates from the community.

Community risk factors
- Community disorganization is evident.
- Community lacks norms that set behavior boundaries.
- Community property is not well maintained.

Secondary Prevention is the response to dealing with risk factors, "How do we prevent a person from being disruptive a second time?"

Consequences such as administrative confrontation, notes sent home to parents, sessions with counselors, and expulsion are prevalent in schools.

In conventional systems of discipline, several agencies, groups, and individuals manage offenders, from school bullies to domestic violence perpetrators.

The approach based on criminal law enforcement procedures is known as "Containment," which is expensive, labor, and time-intensive.

This "out of sight, out of mind" method finger-points and isolates but does not solve the ultimate problem, which may be more profound and enabled by community risk factors. Those add another layer of other organizations and agencies.

All of us have had the top-down, authoritarian model pounded into us starting in Kindergarten.

Habits built around that tendency are hard to shake.

Primary prevention is difficult to quantify because the tactics are conjectural and improve conditions for all people, not only those who exhibit risky behaviors.

What can we do in a cohousing community to prevent disruptive behavior or violence from happening at all?

Protective factors: They are not the opposite of Risk Factors. They are Primary Prevention and buffers against risks associated with disruptive or violent behavior and haven't been studied as extensively as risk factors because they are difficult to measure.

In the community context, it takes a village to create an atmosphere and culture that nurtures protective factors in positive directions rather than negative ones.

The strength-based protective factor approach is more easily implemented if Dunbar's Number is low.

Why?

The more familiar community members are with one another, instead of trying to alleviate malicious behavior, a community can apply protective factors that buffer against harmful actions from happening in the first place.

- The community establishes personal boundaries through shared values, expectations, and norms that emphasize the whole and not the individual.
- The community establishes "cohousing-esque" accountability among all members rather than imposing consequences.
- The community participates in activities that support its "higher purpose" as a diversion from risks.

Restorative Justice is the outside world system that brings together perpetrators, victims, other stakeholders, and the affected community to transform through accountability.

Most community settings don't utilize punishments in the strict sense, and "enforcing" on disruptive or violent people is difficult, if not impossible.

You can't expel them, make them stay after school, lock them up, or whatever.

Conflicts and arguments are dynamic because the roles people take during a conflict change.

- Target (who likely is directly involved)
- Incident Inciter (who may or may not be directly involved in the disruption)
- Retaliator(s) (member(s) who feel harmed by the inciting incident)
- Bystanders (members who may have witnessed the disruptive behavior)
- Intervener (bystander who actively tries to calm down the disruption)

The Target may become the Retaliator. The Incident Inciter may try to be the Target. A Bystander may become a Target if they take on the role of Intervener.

In a cohousing community, the restorative consequence may be as simple as those involved having a conversation among themselves about their accountability to one another since all played multiple roles.

Find Common Ground: There are all kinds of risk-based conflict resolution and conflict avoidance approaches out there. I don't think anybody likes to be confronted about their negative actions. What may be annoying to one may be perfectly good behavior to another.

Unless you practice whatever approach your community has agreed upon, like anything else, effectiveness is better the sooner it becomes a habit.

Any intervention is less effective if the other people involved in an incident don't know what you're trying to achieve through your reframed word choices, for example.

Reframing is the process that made the rounds at SSV. A negative reframe can happen when a good manipulator can gaslight a problem to make it seem like it's the other person's fault.

The "gaslighting" colloquialism enjoyed renewed usage beginning in the mid-2010s. The term loosely defines manipulating someone into questioning their perception of reality. It is based on the title of the film *Gaslight* (1944).

Gaslighting is a form of emotional abuse that can be particularly evident in any relationship, interpersonal or neighbor-to-neighbor.

Say a neighbor is loudly pounding on a neighbor's door and yelling to see if anyone is home. It is incessant and annoys an upstairs neighbor.

"Can you stop that? I have a high anxiety. You don't have to be that noisy!" the bothered resident yells.

"Let me get this straight. Do you mean me using my outside voice? I was just trying to talk to Bessie about how her cat is doing."

"You don't get to gaslight me about this. Besides, you hate cats."

In this case, when one party isn't willing to be accountable, is untruthful, or is manipulative, there is a potential for a "zero-sum" game where there is no compromise if the Incident Inciter continues down a path of no return.

A positive reframing outcome could happen when two arguers spin their wheels with little resolution and reframe to determine if there are common grounds.

There's one orange, and two people want it. Instead of arguing about who saw it first or who wanted it more, each party can state their intention.

"I'm making brunch and want to squeeze out the juice."

"I'm baking a cake and need the rind to make orange zest for the frosting."

In the case of the screaming door pounder, they could have responded, "I didn't have to be that loud. Next time, I'll be more aware of my surroundings."

Both people go away satisfied.

Identifying Bubble Blockers is a protective factor that is a hedge against angst about an issue by identifying potential conflicts ahead of time.

In a community, there may have been a looming or approved decision that takes from the whole to benefit a few, which can create angst.

I call the outcomes "transformational solutions," which is a bit wonky.

Any consequence leveled in a community likely involves many disruptive event contributors who must take ownership of their roles instead of blaming others.

Since disruptions are dynamic and different, many possible role combinations and circumstances exist.

My experience has been that if I played a role in a conflict, by the time I think about the conflict resolution process I was taught, the first reframing action step doesn't come naturally and is not helpful since the moment has passed.

I think the reframing takes practice, unless you have a habit of creating conflicts.

The protective factor approach is preventive because conflicts may happen, but less frequently or disruptively, because everyone involved is accountable to each other, regardless of their interchangeable roles within the same incident.

Ask for Help and Offer Help: During the ensuing years after my deathbed experience, I've become Medicare-eligible, and healthcare isn't the quandary it once was. My memory isn't the steel trap it used to be, and I've learned to do my part to reinvent Superman's American Way by no longer living in denial about my well-being and asking for help.

After being imprisoned in the rehab center and released from captivity in January 2014, I became stronger every day and back into the swing of things.

Being self-employed, I had many ongoing projects.

I think it's also an Asian thing to be self-reliant. Being almost dead taught me that it's okay to ask for help.

When I moved into SSV, I didn't know what that was about until I couldn't take care of myself.

In the cohousing community, we all own our own homes and have agreed to support one another as good neighbors and do chores around the complex.

It's akin to running a family business, and everyone lives on-site.

There's a woman I know in Argentina named Florencia. Latin America is very family-centric. She and her family reside in the same compound that consists of several homes. She's forming her family into a cohousing community.

Flor was adding more structure to her existing family community.

Cohousing tenets, theoretically, are contrary to Superman's American Way of rugged individualism and self-determination.

In the non-cohousing world, asking for help is a sign of weakness. In the cohousing world, it is neither.

I had to learn how to ask for help.

I'm self-employed and have always been able to take care of all my assignments except those due in early 2014.

The last thing I thought I wanted was for people to know that I was flat on my back and unable to finish what I had committed to do.

As far as most people knew, I was fit as a fiddle. I needed help and didn't know how to ask for it, even in desperation.

In the end, a couple of friends and colleagues, Michael and Barbara, kept mud in my entrepreneurial cracks in early 2014.

Asking for help is a constant in cohousing for the good of the whole. There is a fine line between those who ask for help as a way to get out of work and requests that are made out of genuine need.

We're trying to keep the ship moving in the same direction, and it's tough to make that happen if crew members are off doing their own thing, don't instinctively pick up any slack, or forget to perform a task.

Never-ending reminder emails are a reality in a community of seniors with various stages of memory loss.

By the way, have you seen my keys?

Offering help and support is also not as easy as it seems.

"If you need help, give me a call, okay?" is what's asked in the outside world to be polite.

"What can I do to help you now?" is how a cohouser might ask the same question. "You need a jump? I have cables."

"You're in the hospital? I'll stop by and see you when I'm out on my errands today," is another cohousing example of intentionality.

At SSV, for example, I'm on a list of neighbors on-call 24-7 and will contact caregivers and drive a neighbor to the doctor or hospital at any moment.

My next-door neighbor, Henry, and I have a mutual aid agreement. I hailed an ambulance to transport him to the Boulder Community Hospital (BCH) ER for chest pains he had in the middle of the night. I followed and waited until he was admitted. When he was discharged two days later, I gave him a ride home.

It was time for reciprocation.

On Christmas Eve Day 2023, a month after I returned from Panama City, Panama, where I had emergency abdominal surgery, I had a complication from before and pneumonia. I pounded on Henry's door and explained my situation. He grabbed his keys, drove me through the snow, and stuck around BCH until I was either admitted or released.

I ended up spending Christmas at BCH and was discharged two days later.

I pay favors forward and am on the lookout for opportunities to help someone out.

Not every case is a matter of life and death.

I was parked in a Sonic Drive-In stall and left on my headlights three summers ago. After finishing my ice cream, I turned the key to a dead battery. This was before I drove an electric vehicle.

"Do you think I could get a jump?" A woman in an SUV had just finished ordering when I tapped on her door.

Without hesitation, she retrieved one of those self-contained battery chargers and helped me start my VW Sportswagen.

"My husband put these in our cars," she said while hooking up the cables. "I've been wanting to try it out."

That's the latest nonemergency favor I have to pay forward. People are willing to help out in some way and are gracious when assistance is offered.

3d. Climb to the Middle: In the outside world, social climbing to the top is Superman's American Way. In consensus communities like cohousing, the ideal is to claw your way to the middle.

When I was younger, I was one of those chronic overachievers who, without discernment, was always willing to help, join a group, or take on a task.

In my cohousing community, I've dialed that tendency down because it's not essential to be at the top of the pile of a structure that is supposed to be flat and not hierarchical.

Instead, I participate in the outside world and volunteer on several nonprofit organization boards of directors and public boards and commissions.

SSV is where I live, participate at the bare minimum, and check my ego at the Common House door.

Diana and I are transfer students. We moved into SSV two years after the community opened in 2007. SSV was one of a handful of senior cohousing communities.

At that time, my observation was that the founders were feeling their way through collaboration. The culture was tilted more toward power and control by a few.

The place has since become more balanced, with members more accountable and processes more transparent since the community was first occupied.

Every year, for example, everyone's HOA due amounts are known.

The complicated formula is now somewhat simplified. Intellectually, we strive for fairness, but any objective recipe, while "equal," isn't always subjectively "fair."

We're having open discussions about money issues. It's taken going on two decades of community maturity, but everyone is letting loose the reins.

I think overcoming control freak tendencies is the most challenging personal change necessary while reinventing Superman's American Way.

Living in cohousing is an example of the participation dialectic. On one end, it's caring and sharing, and on the other extreme, it's resolving conflicts that arise over self-interests. The synthesis is somewhere in between.

In any business, disagreements arise. Some of my neighbors don't like to refer to the community as a business, even though the SSV community is worth millions and millions of dollars and is self-managed by entrepreneurial residents.

In cohousing, the day-to-day management of the place sometimes results in angst. Irrational decisions can be made flavored by personality conflicts.

Regardless of governance policies in place, there's no accounting for family politics. In this case, cohousing politics. Coalitions are built among neighbors, which can be detrimental and divisive because HOA business becomes personal. Mixing business with family doesn't end well.

In my experience, I've always separated my work from my personal life. Much of living in cohousing is work-related. I learned how to separate myself from the cohousing business.

I don't expect my neighbors to be my best friends or show so much concern they help me into the shower or wipe my butt, but I hope they'll continue to be neighborly.

In his book *Being Mortal: Medicine and What Matters in the End* (2014), author Atul Gawande talks about the importance of hospice, which helps a person be comfortable and provides ideas about navigating through life.

Do I want my friends and family to be hovering over me out of a misguided, self-serving sense of duty when I'm delirious?

Is it quality time to be with me when I take my last breath after you ignored me when I was healthy?

I put myself into self-imposed hospice after I healed up in 2014 while I still have plenty of breaths left and want to be comfortable living life to its fullest.

The side benefit of COVID-19 isolation was convening meetups in Zoom rooms with people around the world.

I've been getting my various bands back together. I'd rather be in touch with family and friends while we still have our wits about us.

4. Down Sizing

We Baby Boomers and older Gen-Xers are now well into our 50s, 60s, and 70s, and trying to figure out how we will care for ourselves now that our kids are scattered all over the country with lives of their own, or in my case, no kids.

The need for safe and decent housing is growing among Baby Boomers who may no longer be working and on some form of retirement income.

There are plenty of downsizing Baby Boomers in preparation for their transitions to different housing options.

Parents no longer need a big house because they kicked the kids out of the nest.

After a whirlwind purge, the junk accumulated over a lifetime in basements and crawl spaces is in the trash, donated to a second-hand store, or repacked, akin to rearranging the deck chairs on the Titanic.

A forming community in Arvada, east of Boulder, invited a panel of speakers to present about how to get rid of the residue of life.

The biggest impediment is undoing the attachment to "things." The bottom line is to hold onto the memories and get rid of the junk.

Those of you who have your parents and grandparents still around spend some time sorting through the family photos and memorabilia.

Write down who is in pictures, the dates, and the surrounding circumstances about how keepsakes were acquired. The box of pictures I inherited spanning three generations is an important memory jogger for memoir research.

I used to think my collections were investments, and they'd appreciate more than mutual funds. I decided to sell it all when I realized my heirs would have no idea where to sell a 1951 Mickey Mantle card or a 1789 George Washington button.

I could have made more money retailing it piece by piece, but that would entail packing, shipping and resulted in twenty or thirty bucks per sale and taking the rest of my dwindling time on earth.

An externality that helped me decide was the Marshall urban wildfire that incinerated over 1,000 homes and businesses in East Boulder County on December 30, 2021.

Residents had no time to gather their valuables and lost everything. I didn't want to put myself in that situation.

As it turned out, my stuff had appreciated since I acquired the bulk of my collection that spanned the 19th century through the 1960s when prices were very low. I liquidated my extensive baseball and political memorabilia collections in two bulk sales.

The photos I took of my New York Yankees cards and campaign buttons are all that remain to remind me of my erstwhile hobbies.

Each SSV household has one storage space in the basement. One couple are hoarders, and their boxes are creeping into other residents' spaces. Plus, they have an off-campus storage unit.

I lugged all my college textbooks around with me for years. When high-powered telescopes found rings around Jupiter, I got rid of them all.

I figured out that famous people are the only ones who have any business keeping their stuff after I visited Elvis's Graceland estate in Memphis. I knew Elvis was famous, but I didn't realize he was THAT famous.

When I'm dead and gone, nobody is going to care about the Lander, Wyoming Centennial poster from 1984 that's stashed in a box.

If you're a potential cohouser, as a family, how to deal with your stuff is important, but also talk about your future and not just about estate planning but, more importantly, about how holiday traditions and celebrations will be preserved.

My sister sorted out our Christmas tree ornaments and other holiday ephemera. I've missed two Christmases when I was in the hospital. Other than those, I put up a tree and don't open packages until Christmas morning.

I'll keep up with my Christmas traditions for as long as I'm alive, and then that'll be it.

Before you have family meetings like this, I suggest taking some yoga classes.

Looser hips and thighs have made me more aware of my root *chakra* – bring on the holiday havoc!

Lower-Priced Housing Shortage: Besides housing-stressed seniors, other low-moderate income households need help finding safe and lower-cost rental or ownership housing options.

I don't see myself slowing down anytime soon since I'm still writing books and making movies. Those pursuits aren't back-breaking but keep me active enough.

I don't consider what I do to be "work."

Intentional communities that include cohousing can help meet the impending senior citizen lower-priced housing shortage.

Collaborative living is also linked to decreasing social isolation. Loneliness is as deadly as smoking 15 cigarettes per day.

According to a 2015 U.S. Aging Survey, 58 percent of seniors have lived in the same home for at least the past 20 years.

Even though people ideally want to stay in one place, there is anecdotal evidence about future uncertainty.

"Who will take care of you when you get old?" I asked in a facebook post while researching this story.

I was surprised at the 2,000+ engagements and 850 responses that ranged from "myself" to "nobody" to "I don't know" to "maybe one of my kids" to "my cohousing neighbors."

If you're an "empty nester" in a large home, one option is to downsize by selling it. You may or may not be able to purchase something in the community where you've lived for 30 or 40 years.

Another option is to keep the home and convert it into a cooperative house, like the TV sitcom *Golden Girls* (1985 - 1992), and rent out rooms as a hedge against loneliness.

I don't own a large house, and can live independently. A time will come when I will need assistance or be unable to take care of myself.

Jim and Brownie, my across-the-sidewalk neighbors, are experimenting with a part-time caregiver who lives in their basement apartment. Jim suggested that the community should consider circuit-riding caregivers who would either live on or off campus.

Lifecare managers, gerontologists, and social workers believe a strong correlation exists between safe, lower-priced housing and keeping seniors healthy through informal and formal caregiving.

A longer life doesn't always translate into a better quality of life. No one knows this better than the millions of adult children caring for their parents who struggle to remain in family homes and communities not designed for the challenges of aging.

Those challenges include limited cash to pay for services, long travel distances, and non-existent or limited relationships between parents and their children.

Historically, seniors aged in their homes for as long as possible with support from family and informal caregivers until they died or health conditions deteriorated to the point that hospital or nursing home care was necessary.

My dad ended up passing in the hospital, although my sister and I made an effort to get him into hospice care in his home. My mom died from a brain aneurysm while sleeping.

These data are now flipped. Atul Gawande observes that most people die in the hospital or a long-term care facility rather than in the privacy of their own bed.

The circumstances of where, how, and with whom people grow old are changing.

Baby Boomers are redefining how they live out their lives, ranging from the cooperative housemate households to high-rise artist-centered apartment buildings.

We are breaking down old stereotypes and societal rules, imagining new visions of great places to grow old, and doing it better by living in cohousing communities.

Since the average age of the SSV community residents is 73 years, up from the late 60s when Diana and I joined, the people who now live at SSV are different from my original neighbors because of housing turnover.

Our shared values are similar to when I first joined, but they've been tweaked over the years to reflect the new community character, which has evolved toward more creativity.

At SSV, we're much better at consensus decision-making. How we operate and maintain common spaces such as a Common House is also changing, and the community is in discussion about altering participation levels because we're aging.

Most of the heavy lifting, like snow removal and lawn maintenance, is contracted out, as well as the lighter-duty Common House cleaning. Community participation these days consists of how to boss around the contractors.

Some residents can no longer bend over to weed the garden or plant. I'm on the Finance and Legal Team, which requires zero physical work.

I plan to stay at SSV until I die. I hope my death happens quickly due to a brain aneurysm in my sleep.

Continuing Care Residential Community (CCRC):
Five SSV households with adequate financial resources recently moved into a CCRC at the same time.

Cohousing living is a good way for future CCRC residents to become accustomed to community life rather than joining cold turkey.

I like the continuous care concept. A resident can start in independent living, move to assisted living, and eventually to long-term care.

I can also foresee relationships among separate independent living, assisted living, and long-term care facilities tying themselves together by adding the cohousing secret sauce.

For decades, CCRCs have offered older adults, usually aged 65 and older, an innovative and independent lifestyle that differs from other housing and care options.

Residents with experience in a cohousing community could seamlessly transition into another independent living situation, assisted living, nursing home, or a CCRC.

Experience gained from living in cohousing could be the entry point to a CCRC. I don't know if this has happened, but a CCRC could build relationships with cohousing communities to be resident "feeders" who transition into continuous care.

The main limitation of retrofitting an existing CCRC is one of control. CCRCs are typically managed "top-down" as opposed to resident-directed.

When cohousers move into a CCRC, depending on their entry point, whether independent, assisted, or in long-term care, they are accustomed to collaborating with others.

A person who has lived independently without the benefit of nurtured relationships within a community may feel they are losing independence instead of being separate but together.

I witnessed this in an assisted living community. A new resident from out of town was admitted by her children.

She had a hissy fit about being left by her family in an "institution."

In my case, the Manor Care rehabilitation center also provided long-term care.

Whether they knew it or not, many aspects of cohousing were integrated into their social activities.

During my two-week stay, I checked out as much of the programming as I could.

I was there just before the Super Bowl, and one of the social activities was painting Denver Bronco art.

It was fun to socialize with others, even though I was the only man among a table of women, most of whom were long-term care residents.

CCRCs allow seniors to convert home equity or other assets into a place to live and receive daily living services and health care that keeps monthly expenditures more stable, like the meal plan in my college dorm.

A traditional CCRC isn't for everybody. There are also stand-alone independent, assisted, and long-term living facilities that offer housing for Medicaid-eligible tenants.

The National Long-Term Care Survey (NLTCS) is a nationally representative sample of community and institutionalized populations.

It is longitudinal in that sample persons join the survey once they reach 65 years of age and stay in the study until they die or are unable to follow up.

The NLTCS data from 2004 has not been updated in 20 years, but the trend is that while CCRC residents are among the oldest and sickest population, they have the highest incomes that average between $40,000 and $45,000, probably much higher now.

Compare that to those in assisted or independent living who report average incomes of $24,000.

CCRCs are a tried-and-true lifestyle option for some seniors, particularly those with higher income and net worth, but what about everyone else?

Applying cohousing principles to other housing configurations, intentionally developing relationships among neighbors, and subsequent sharing of tasks and care for one another.

That experience could delay the need for other independent and assisted living types.

When buying into and living at a CCRC, which is costly, residents exchange their home equity and assets for housing and daily meals.

Entrance fees range from about $20,000 to more than $500,000 or even $1,000,000, based on an area's cost of living. These fees are unaffordable to most people.

We're all getting older every day. Unfortunately, for many young people, say, under 50, the prospects of aging aren't on their radar screens.

"I fell down and can't get up" is what GenXers hear when they answer a phone call from a parent.

It's not until then, or when the "Join AARP" membership junk mail arrives, that they begin to take notice.

Home living conditions have a considerable impact on the health of seniors living with long-term illness and their abilities to live independently.

According to the Aging Life Care Association, care managers and geriatricians are often called upon to advise families about where their aging family members who have developed illnesses or disability can live.

Seniors and their families now seek more information about the relationship between safe, price-efficient housing and health.

At-risk older people on fixed incomes with no familial safety net are more likely to be living in a non-decent rental or owner-occupied home.

Limited data: The 4th annual 2015 United States Aging Survey, also dated, conducted by the National Association of Area Agencies on Aging, the National Council on Aging, and United Healthcare, examined senior perspectives on aging and how communities can better support an increasing, longer-living senior population.

The survey included a nationally representative sample of 1,650 Americans 60 and older and professionals who work closely with them. These data support a need for collaborative communities.

Financial concerns: The top financial concerns among the respondents are the increasing cost of living, 28 percent, and unexpected medical expenses, 24 percent.

Maintaining health: Professionals and seniors agree that maintaining good health as they age is essential. They named eating healthy, 91 percent and 72 percent, respectively; maintaining a positive attitude, 86 percent and 72 percent; and getting enough sleep, 79 percent and 67 percent.

Staying at home and independent: When asked what concerns they have about living independently, 42 percent of seniors say they are most concerned about becoming a burden to others, 41 percent say experiencing memory loss, and 34 percent say being unable to get out of the house or drive.

Community Support: Of the sample, 59 percent of seniors say that young people today are less supportive of seniors than previous generations, 24 percent see the same levels of support, and 12 percent say young people are more supportive of older adults; 47 percent, (down from 54 percent in 2014 and 49 percent in 2013) and 37 percent of the professionals say their community is doing enough to prepare for the needs of retiring Baby Boomers.

Community Formation Steps: Cohousing, particularly Coho Ultra-Lite, can fill the cost-efficient and lower-cost housing gap.

Most cohousing communities are multigenerational but evolve into senior communities over time because of people who age-in-place.

There are close to a dozen established senior-only cohousing communities, and more are in the forming stages.

Research points to a variety of cohousing benefits. The most often mentioned benefits relate to reducing social isolation.

The cohousing secret sauce provides for intentional socializing, neighborly support when under the weather, chore sharing, expertise sharing, and having neighbors who share similar interests.

Retrofit Coho Ultra-Lite can more immediately help fill the lower-cost housing gap and likely meet the needs of marginalized community members.

The eldercare industrial complex is well established.

Breaking into that with a housing product that takes away corporate control is a thick glass ceiling to shatter.

I know of a lifecare manager in Gloucester, Massachusetts, who is studying how to pour cohousing secret sauce over an assisted living facility.

The social support that cohousing offers may be beneficial for an aging population.

Senior cohousing has received recent attention as a model to support well-being and age in place through emotional support and mutual assistance activities (e.g., errands, driving, cooking, or walking with a neighbor), downsizing their lives, and personal safety.

Plan Out Your Community: The steps you would follow when thinking through any cohousing community project follow the same basic steps.

There are many templates and business planning tools out there. Pick one that resonates with you and your projects.

Your community story premise should be the first step in expanding out to an outline, synopsis, and a full business plan.

Adapt any template to meet the unique needs of you and your community.

Does My Project Make Sense? Discuss and agree upon community values and, perhaps, a higher purpose, which would fill the need to walk their community values talk while participating in service projects.

Whether you're three or thirty people, come up with a name and "elevator speech" identifying the community.

If you're starting as an Ultra-Lite and evolving into Coho Stout or Lite, your feasibility study may include transitions from one form to another.

That transition analysis would include evaluating existing housing stock quantities and prices if you're thinking about building new or acquiring buildings.

Referring to yourselves as a "bunch of housemates" doesn't say much about your community story.

Your group may add a higher purpose, say, community service, that creates cohesiveness among members.

That could be a common spiritual practice or volunteering at various local nonprofits.

Maybe you're a group of accountants who provide income tax filing assistance at a domestic violence shelter.

Once you kick the can down the road a few blocks, check your state laws about HOA regulations.

You will find that non-cohousing HOAs do not mirror collaborative governance very well. Traditional HOAs have centralized power and control in a board of directors and lots of voting.

Save this step until later because conforming cohousing declarations with state laws is a chore.

When you get closer to formally organizing, the CohoUS website that provides workshop and training program schedules can point you in the right direction.

How Much Does All This Cost? For Coho Ultra-Lite, there will likely be ordinary expenses that relate to community activities, transportation coordination, shared meals, intra-community communication, and a fee structure to pay for all or part of these expenses.

For revenues, you'll likely have dues of some sort. I think having a "buy-in" from members also provides a sense of ownership and belonging.

Community values and mission are implemented through the budget by teams.

An example would be the SSV Steering Team, equivalent to a board of directors that derives its authority from the community.

Separate teams under the Steering Team's direction would organize social events, manage buildings and grounds, keep track of finances and legal matters.

The entire community approves the budget, or any action for that matter, by consensus. The steering team ratifies community actions also by consensus.

Coho Stout communities require more hands-on participation by the community.

The developer likely holds the project in a corporate structure during the development phase.

The prospective members are often included since they assume some of the upfront financial risks.

Coho Lite projects are generally developed separately from the forming community.

Community members arrange for traditional home financing, purchase their home from the developer, and subsequently join the HOA.

What's This Thing Look Like? Coho Stout projects require the most "hands-on" participation from the potential residents directly involved in the community's design and layout.

Coho Stout communities are the subject of most "how-to-build" cohousing literature.

Lite communities are more developer-driven, and the project is less customizable.

The developer provides potential home buyers with a list of limited choices for carpets and other interior finishes.

If you're making an Ultra-Lite community and sharing a big house, there might be issues with designating common spaces and storage.

Ultra-Lite residents may want to alter room configurations to add space to the kitchen.

Your group may need to finish the basement to add more bedrooms or a common area.

Suppose you're purchasing in an existing condo community or renting units in an apartment complex.

In those cases, there likely will be some role for a design professional and contractor to retrofit your building correctly.

A retrofit may include renovating an existing dwelling unit into a shared space with a guest room and shared kitchen, which was the case at Boulder Creek cohousing in Colorado and Genesee Garden in Michigan.

Identify resident needs and how the "site" functions in an existing physical development like a condo association, apartment complex, or households dispersed within a given boundary.

"Common spaces," which may not be literally common but function in common, should be considered and determined. These may be in private homes for shared meals and meetings, civic spaces, churches, or libraries.

There are plenty of individuals who are interested in cohousing. Some of you may have formed into a group that has begun the traditional cohousing process.

Maybe you've bumped into obstacles that include lack of money, no suitable land, and design professionals only willing to give so much free upfront service.

Group members may drop out because they can no longer wait for the community to get off the ground.

There are well-documented stories about community member attrition.

In our case, Diana and I couldn't wait the three or four years it would take for the Wild Sage Cohousing community to complete, and we bought a townhouse a block away.

If constructing smaller, cost-efficient, lower-priced housing was profitable, there would be no shortage. There are various reasons why this is true.

Obstacles: I'll mention three potential challenges. Your experiences will vary since all counties, cities, towns, and neighborhoods differ.

Local government: If you're not picky about where you plunk down your project, places with wider open zoning and building codes are the paths of least resistance.

Wherever you choose, remember to follow the rules that best fit your project.

Zoning changes and requests for exceptions to the code take time and involve political decision-making by Planning Commissions, City Councils, or both.

As cities get larger, the level of "professionalism" becomes more complex, and as such, costs go up, and city staff scrutiny increases.

You may want to engage a real estate or design expert to give you a hand. You'll likely find someone who will provide some service on speculation or as a favor.

Regardless of your community's size, the municipal or county staff members are generally very willing to help you through the process.

Banks: Depending on the cohousing configuration, banks are at greater ease as a project becomes simpler.

Coho Stout entails a group of people who chip in to spread the risk, possibly with a developer.

This financing configuration can be problematic for a bank that wants to minimize risk. Bankers may be cautious about loaning money to many people with various credit histories.

Usually, there is some corporate structure like a limited liability corporation (LLC) where each person assumes their fair share of risk.

Because project owners seek outside investment, some state governments consider this financing arrangement an offering of securities.

Check with your state's Secretary of State or Attorney General to learn how securities and exchange laws may apply to your project.

For a Coho Stout development, "lay developers" may be intimately involved with the land purchase, contracting for design services, and construction financing.

If you want to avoid the brain damage that can go along with a cohousing community development, Coho Lite projects are developer-driven.

Banks like to work with developers and development companies with proven records of buying land and building houses, as was the case with the Bloomington Cohousing project in Indiana.

The burning souls can spend their time doing the fun stuff like coming up with the community story, attracting members, and planning activities.

In the case of an owner-occupied Coho Lite community, each resident would arrange for their financing.

Banks understand how to write mortgages for single-family houses.

The least risky approach is Coho Ultra-Lite. Members devote more time to forming the community first.

The group can begin their community by deciding how they want to live.

Maybe they'll want to chip in and purchase an existing four-plex or eight-plex, rent in the same place, or act as a community from their individual homes.

It could be that after forming their group, Coho Stout or Coho Lite are better options.

Neighborhood: Cohousing is just starting to become known in mainstream society.

Intentional communities have been stereotyped as hippie communes. That couldn't be farther from reality.

In cohousing communities, there are no shared economies. People live in private homes and enjoy the benefits of shared amenities.

That's no different from a "normal" apartment building with a swimming pool or condominium complex with a clubhouse and tennis courts.

Some projects require neighborhood meetings when you go through the local government approval process. When terms like "high-density," "affordable," or "low-moderate income" are bantered about, Superman's American Way boils those terms down to stereotypes about poor people, high traffic, junk cars, and lower property values.

"Everyone needs to live someplace," is a comment heard at a public hearing about an apartment building proposed that abuts a single-family neighborhood. "Build those affordable houses someplace else."

I think most people understand the importance of lower-cost housing and why homes need to be provided for all, but "Not in My Back Yard" (NIMBY).

A researcher from Boston University studied the role local government plays in preventing housing construction in Massachusetts.

The study focused on planning and zoning boards that play prominent roles in implementing land use regulations throughout the United States.

When city officials ask neighbors of housing projects to comment, those who attend present overwhelmingly more negative perspectives about additional housing than the average citizen. NIMBY proponents are more likely to be economically advantaged or white.

The findings suggest that even though antidevelopment forces are fewer in number, they participate at a rate greater than new housing development proponents, who are larger in numbers but more diffuse.

There's an urban myth that new high-density property or low-cost housing causes values to decline.

Red-lining: That perspective is a throwback to "red-lining" and the market-based formation of pockets of poverty.

In the 1960s, a sociologist named John McKnight coined the term "red-lining" to describe what turned out to be a discriminatory practice that created geographic boundaries where banks could avoid investing based on community demographics.

Congress formed the Federal Housing Administration (FHA) as a part of the National Housing Act of 1934.

President Roosevelt and his New Deal FHA policies intended to provide banks with criteria to guide safe lending practices ended up accelerating inner-city decay in areas inhabited mainly by lower-income minority households.

In 1935, the Federal Home Loan Bank Board, through the Home Owners Loan Corporation, evaluated 239 cities and designated areas on "residential security maps" to indicate the real-estate investment risk levels:

- Type A "Newer" suburbs most desirable for lending outlined in green.
- Type B "Desirable" neighborhoods outlined in blue.
- Type C "Declining" older areas outlined in yellow.
- Type D "Risky" communities considered poor investments outlined in red.

Based on these risk assumptions, racial segregation and urban decline were two externalities that arose.

While red-lining is not prevalent today, its legacies are urban areas in decay and in need of revitalization or redevelopment.

Another unintended consequence is the unfounded belief that lower-priced, cost-efficient housing drives down property values.

Well-designed high-density developments that fit in with the surrounding housing stock's character do not lower home value.

When I worked for Habitat for Humanity, we built a few homes on infill lots in mature neighborhoods.

My goal was to build smaller houses that looked indistinguishable from the surrounding housing stock.

There were standard Habitat house plans, but the contractor adapted them with exteriors similar to those of the neighbors' homes.

I was a member of the city of Boulder Planning Board. Occasionally, controversial projects would come before us for consideration, like a transitional rental housing project next to the Boulder Homeless Shelter.

The xenophobic NIMBY neighbors came out in droves and feared that the lower-priced rental housing translated into pedophilia and high crime.

That perspective astounded me.

If your cohousing project requires waivers from a "by-right" project and approvals from appointed and elected officials, be prepared to present a good story during public hearings.

Planning and zoning officials could care less if you have community meals and dry your wet garments on clotheslines or if you grow organic arugula in the courtyard raised beds.

All they want to know is how your project fits into their rules and regulations.

De-commodify Housing: I'm a Baby Boomer and will focus this discussion on housing as an investment following World War II.

In the context of cohousing, most existing communities are of the Coho Stout variety, which entails high levels of front-end investment into land and housing construction that takes many years to build at the cost of millions of dollars.

Coho Stout and Lite are out of most people's price ranges.

Superman's American Way views housing as a commodity. Commodities are generally associated with raw materials and agricultural products bought and sold based on future value.

De-commodifying housing, particularly rental housing, is a lofty goal. The market doesn't respond well to caps on how much money they can earn from the financial investments and rents.

If there's a housing market that de-commodifies housing, it would be that of cohousers.

Cohousers place a high value on community relationships and, in that respect, reinvent Superman's American Way.

In the SSV HOA, the higher-value homes have more to gain in terms of property appreciation than the smaller, cost-efficient, lower-priced but deed-restricted homes.

"We need to add the new trees because my property value will increase" is the commodity-based perspective on improving the cohousing community shared space.

"We need to add the new trees because they will provide more shade for kids to play under, and as a side benefit, our property value will go up" is the "de-commodified community good" reasoning behind improving the cohousing commonly shared space.

Cohousers maintain their properties, which, theoretically, flattens costs. In traditional housing, operation cost fluctuations concern rental property investors.

Cohousers are more likely to alter their perspectives, consider their homes as places to live, and only view their homes as commodities at the time of sale.

The Coho Stout model is around ownership. A different mindset does not mean abandoning reserving funds for major long-term replacements and repairs. Nor does de-commodification of homes mean trashing out the shared spaces and Common House.

De-commodification does mean community improvement decisions are made based on improving interpersonal relationships.

Coho Ultra-Lite communities are best suited to be de-commodified. Rental communities sprinkled with the cohousing secret sauce can take the profit motive out of the project.

Like Boulder Creek Cohousing, renters can build limited equity and decrease costs by joining together and maintaining and managing the community by building strong interpersonal relationships.

Senior community development is on the rise because Baby Boomers and older possess the accumulated or inherited wealth needed to buy into a Coho Stout community.

For other seniors, though, safe and lower-priced housing is getting to be inaccessible with out-of-sight prices because of the lack of supply.

Local governments and lenders view houses as market-based commodities rather than public goods.

Minneapolis was the first major city in the United States to eliminate the single-family zoning district. Low-density housing occupied three-quarters of residential property.

Exclusionary zoning: Local government ordinances specifically established residential zoning districts that only allowed large single-family dwelling units on huge lots in response to a 1917 U.S. Supreme Court (SCOTUS) case, *Buchanan v. Warley*.

An African-American named William Warley submitted an offer to buy property from a white owner named Charles Buchanan.

Buchanan, the seller, argued that he couldn't complete the sale because the City of Louisville wouldn't let him.

Buchanan argued that the Louisville ordinance that enforced racial segregation in Louisville and prevented him from selling his property to Warley was unconstitutional.

The SCOTUS ruled that the Louisville, Kentucky city ordinance motive to separate races was an inappropriate exercise of police power.

Local governments answered with *de facto* segregation by approving low-density zoning districts that prescribed large homes on large lots.

Permitted housing would be expensive and, therefore, out of the price range of potential African-American buyers.

The low-density, single-family zoning district has had a solid 100-year run.

In response to the exclusionary zoning district, the Minneapolis up-zoning is designed to narrow the gap in homeownership rates between whites (59 percent) and African Americans (21 percent).

Regardless of land use designation changes, the housing industrial complex is a tough nut to crack.

Rather than changing zoning codes that would encourage market-based solutions that provide lower-cost housing, local governments and the private nonprofit sector have come up with creative workarounds.

Those include community land trusts formed by charitable people who donate land or sell the land at a lower cost to get tax write-off benefits. Prices are lower because owners essentially pay no land cost because the houses are built on trust property.

Wealthy investors can apply Low-Income Housing Tax Credits (LIHTC) to lower the cost of development projects.

The HUD-administered program benefited close to 50,000 projects consisting of 3.2 million dwelling units between 1987 and 2015.

Outright grant funds are available from local governments or private foundations that can lower housing projects' prices.

Superman's American Way evolved after veterans returned from World War II, and they and their families flooded the suburbs with new housing construction. That included G.I. Bill housing benefits for my friend Tom, who obtained financing for our 3003 Club cooperative house in Gillette, Wyoming.

Homeowners have always viewed their houses as investments. Improvements made to a home increase the property's value.

When I was a kid, a family project was adding a bomb shelter in the basement for Civil Defense, but it also added to the home's value, particularly during the Cold War.

My bedroom was moved to the basement to give me more space and turn the house from three to four bedrooms.

The burning souls planning the Ultra-Lite big-box store retrofit community in Colorado Springs is an example of how the city government can collaborate with the business community to solve the lower-priced housing shortage.

The collaborative outcome allows for more flexibility in their zoning code to allow for innovative mixed-use projects, as the proposed Ultra-Lite retrofitted vacant big-box retail building.

Working around the housing industrial complex by encouraging more government-owned housing, rent, and purchase price controls, efforts should also promote market-based solutions through regulatory reform.

Epilogue: The Power of c*OM*unification

Cohousing Nation, by definition, reinvents Superman's American Way" that balances the good of the community over that of the individual, accepts all people as different, welcomes and values everyone, and exercises power through collaboration and consensus among all.

As such, I'm convinced that intentional community advocates have the potential to get up off the couch and put in the hard work it takes to bridge cultural divides that continue to plague our country today.

The average cohouser has at least some social justice blood running through their veins. I think organized cohousers can collectively make social change happen.

Once the conflict about what kind of kitchen countertops to choose is resolved and arguments about pets are over, what if cohousers turned their attention to closing cultural divides and advocating for lower-cost cohousing?

I estimate 30,000 cohousers live in a community or forming one and are gatekeepers who work together and ally with marginalized groups.

The inclusion of diverse people organically brings about additional lower-cost housing as the dominant culture becomes more inclusive based on what I call c*OM*unification.

I looked up the definition of *OM*. The Sanskrit concept has ethereal meanings and interpretations. My version of *OM* is the audible drone of the universe and includes everything – past, present, future, beginning, middle, and end.

c*OM*unification focuses on how changing individual personal values can balance cultural and societal power and privilege, which is easier thought about than realized.

Before Superman came around, the "American Way" had deep Western European and Christian roots.

Regardless of your spiritual tradition or lack thereof, you've probably heard this metaphor referenced in Babylonian spirituality, Judaism, Islam, and Christianity.

It's about a camel passing through the eye of a needle that is more likely than a rich man to enter paradise or become humble.

In the Christian version, in Matthew 19:21-24, a rich guy asks Jesus what it takes to be a better person.

"Follow the commandments. Give all your possessions to the poor," Jesus responds.

The rich guy is bummed out and walks away, unwilling to give up what it takes to be a better person.

Not that there's anything wrong with Superman's "American Way" based on rugged individualism, cultural divides narrowed by assimilation, and quests for power and control.

Reinventing Superman's American Way means that a societal alternative needs to evolve along through a collaborative approach.

Considering the American traditions around slavery and general xenophobia towards Asian and Muslim immigrants, that's a challenge.

The earliest story I looked up happened in 1526 when 500 settlers from Spain kidnapped 100 Africans to a colony in what are now the states of South Carolina and Georgia.

The invaders also kidnapped and enslaved 70 indigenous tribal members.

Public awareness of differences among people, particularly since the Civil Rights Act of 1964, enflamed simmering racist attitudes that continue to exist today.

I think people want to change their ingrained perspectives and do what's right, but based on the audiences I've met over the years, most people don't know what to do or where to start.

Personal change doesn't happen overnight and, like anything else that requires better skills, takes practice.

People aren't exactly crazy about letting go of personal privilege.

Considering America has a 334-year history of enslaving people (1526 to 1865), that's more than double the 160-year history since President Abraham Lincoln's Emancipation Proclamation (1863 to 2020).

There have been actions of social change that have occurred since the Civil War. The 19th Amendment gave women the right to vote for one, but reinventing the American Way won't happen overnight.

Public policy evolved faster than mainstream society has been able to keep up.

At the same time, other government actions exacerbated racial and ethnic injustice.

There is a long-standing national culture that institutionalized racial homogeneity.

President George Washington's administration established the United States Naturalization Law of March 26, 1790, that limited citizenship to immigrants who were "free White persons of good character.

The U.S. Congress passed the Chinese Exclusion Act in 1882. President Chester Arthur signed the Act that provided a 10-year moratorium on Chinese labor immigration to the United States.

The Immigration Act of 1924 prohibited Japanese immigration and set tighter quotas on immigration from all other countries.

Most recently, the Muslim bans that occurred by executive order by the outgoing 45th U.S. President are the latest blatant forms of xenophobia.

The police-involved killing of George Floyd and others during the COVID-19 pandemic is further evidence of racism baked into governmental institutions that mirror the dominant American culture.

I think that part of that cultural reinvention lies in the lap of cohousing, which is a market-based solution that bridges cultural divides.

CohoUS sponsored a web-based conference about community inclusion that resulted in a series of national discussions about racial and ethnic justice.

There are as many different approaches, from ranting and chanting at marches to one-on-one conversations to cultural competency, as there are burning souls to herd the cats and make social change happen.

Cohousing brings individuals together to form communities that agree on a set of shared values played out in the relationships that develop through participation.

What if the 320 cohousing existing and forming communities joined together around a racial and ethnic justice issue and made change happen in their cities, counties, and states?

The collective energy of 30,000 people could have a significant impact on closing cultural divides.

In this book, I talked about how cohousing neighbors form relationships by committing to be part of a community for mutual benefit.

Cohousing, whether you choose Coho Stout, Lite, or Ultra-Lite, all cultivate cultures of sharing and caring.

Design features, whether in several detached homes or one building, promote frequent interaction and close relationships.

Cohousing residents balance privacy and community by choosing their levels of community participation.

Decision-making is participatory and based on consensus. Self-management empowers residents, builds relationships, and can save money.

Shared values are what bind cohousing community residents together. Their participation and collaboration actualize shared values by walking the talk.

The cohousing brand is just beginning to be mainstream.

There is an ilk of the public, mostly Baby Boomers and older, who experienced the Cold War and repositioned the cohousing conversation by clumping cohousing together with communes and creeping socialism.

Cohousing isn't about overthrowing the government or tossing out social norms but instead reacting to how the general market is changing.

Theoretically, cohousing neighborhoods can be less expensive and where residents collaboratively get along in higher-density neighborhoods and share resources (16 households don't each need a lawnmower).

If you define cohousing as neighbors residing in "private dwellings" rather than "private houses," the configuration can be even less expensive and can include housing coops with lockable rooms.

In Superman's American Way, rugged individualists and free-market capitalists are unwilling to share their wealth, and as such, the market reaction should be toward c*OM*unification.

As of June 2018, *Forbes Magazine* reported that 44.2 million people owed $1.52 trillion in student debt, which averaged $38,390 per *alumnus*.

Baby Boomers, GenXers, and Millennials have more in common than they think and could stand to learn from one another.

Baby Boomers and those older on fixed incomes, maybe with little inherited wealth or accumulated savings, also seek lower-priced housing options.

Because of student loans and personal debt, the children and grandchildren of Baby Boomers can't afford nor have the desire to live in the large homes in the suburbs championed by their parents.

My observation is that Millennials and GenXers who are a generation or two removed from World War II are more likely to accept individual differences and be more supportive of the collective good, all out of a need to survive.

Millennials and GenXers are candidates to live in de-commodified housing and reinvent Superman's American Way.

Parents and their students errantly believed that a college education would be the path to a glorious, high-paying job. A graduate walks across the stage and is handed their diploma along with $146,000 of college debt that will saddle them until they are old and gray.

I'm walking proof of that. What Baby Boomer in their right mind would go to grad school when they are old enough to know better? I was laid off from a job in 2004, and lucky that student loans and unemployment benefits kept me afloat for two years. It took me 14 years to pay off the loan.

Millennials, Gen-Xers, and Baby Boomers have more in common than they may think. On average, the 2023 debt for a Millennial was $49,000, a Gen-Xer $61,000, and a Baby Boomer $62,000.

The three generations would benefit from intergenerational Coho Ultra Lite de-commodified housing options. The American standard continues to be owning a detached single-family dwelling on a private lot.

That isn't sustainable. I listened to a story on National Public Radio that included interviews with affordable housing advocates who poo-pooed children having to live with their parents longer. Renting living quarters with roommates also detracted from Superman's American Way.

Reinventing Superman's American Way repositions a home as a building in which we live, not an investment. A home could be a shared house or living in your parent's basement.

Owners should only commodify their homes when it's time to sell their houses and move.

The cohousing brand of community development is a hedge against unchecked gentrification, which is one of those jargony terms that get thrown around and used in various contexts.

I define gentrification as when people or businesses seek out real estate deals, purchase urban property that may or may not be distressed, and update them without much collaboration with existing neighbors.

When revitalizing an area in relative decline, a developer using the cOMunification approach would meet with area formal and informal leaders ahead of time.

Rather than buying buildings, razing, and displacing residents and businesses with Starbucks and Whole Foods, the developer would establish partnerships that engage the existing shopkeepers and share the wealth so they can remain.

I presented a cohousing workshop in Nashville sponsored by the Tennessee Housing Development Agency (THDA). One of the participants in my cultural competency session was a guy who worked for THDA.

He was interested in pouring the cohousing secret sauce over a housing rehabilitation project in Nashville where strong extended families lived within the same neighborhood.

His idea was to collaborate with the neighbors to renovate existing homes rather than scraping off the housing stock and replacing it.

The concept is to maintain a sense of community rather than tearing one down and replacing it with another.

cOMunification cuts into profits, but that's part of the de-commodification paradigm shift.

Cohousing communities consist of predominantly liberal, highly educated, high-income Caucasians with high perceived social class and 70 percent of the time a woman.

Based on those demographics, the typical cohouser, in my mind, is inclined to bridge cultural divides by reinventing Superman's American Way from the inside out.

That is to say, members of the dominant culture who live in cohousing have agreed among themselves to change their perspectives about consumerism, competition, and cultural dominance.

I think marginalized groups should engage cohousers and their communities to be allies and help bridge cultural divides in American society.

Without cultural brokerage, efforts by dominant culture cohousers to encourage marginalized people to join their relatively closed communities is an uphill climb.

The result of c*OM*unification, by definition, is an attitudinal shift by members of the dominant culture who have agreed to increase cultural diversity in the broader culture, one cohousing community at a time.

Cohousing c*OM*unification happens through public policy that reflects the interests of a continually evolving pluralistic culture that reinvents Superman's American Way.

- There's a balance between the group and the individual.
- Smaller and less are better, but all share in the abundance that isn't always about bigger and more.
- Decisions are made by consensus, giving a voice to all, including minority positions.
- There is a recognition that everyone is different, and all are included as themselves.

Since our nation's founding, America has been a pluralistic culture despite early government efforts to conquer the West by killing Native Americans, slaughtering bison, and limiting immigration, particularly from Asia.

In the 18th century, J. Hector St. John de Crevecoeur wrote in his *Letters from an American Farmer* (1782) a "Melting Pot" metaphorically mixes races and ethnicities who learn English and assimilate into homogenous Americans.

I listened to a lecturer when I was in graduate school at the University of Colorado – Denver. She said that societal homogeneity would happen because of interracial marriage. I argued that her assumption that everyone would self-identify as white was wrong.

"That might have been true before the Civil War when the offspring of a slave and white owner were classified as white, but that's not true now," I said. "People aren't forced to be who they are."

That was also true during racial segregation when the melting pot contained white cheeses like Swiss, Edam,

Gouda, and Feta. They blended to make a mixed pot of white cheese.

Immigrants from Europe who all looked like each other had Superman's American Way ahead of them after learning English and otherwise assimilating.

These days, the country has become racially and ethnically multicultural due to immigration. While learning English, the American first language is desirable. The promise of a good American life for brown-skinned people isn't a practical reality.

Today, the blended food metaphor would be more like a "Tossed Salad" consisting of separate fixings like *frijoles*, *cassavas*, *napa* cabbage, and all kinds of lettuce unified with a common dressing.

That common dressing is the "Cohousing c*OM*unification" secret sauce, soon available at a farmer's market near you.

-30-

Made in the USA
Columbia, SC
18 March 2024